Sometimes it seems that everything we do should be labeled "Life's Most Embarrassing Moments." Just when we're starting to relax, something happens and we find ourselves flat on our faces — flopped again. Things like...

- forgetting the lines in the school play
- discovering that you're the only girl in your group who's never been on a date...not even a double date
- ripping out your pants in the seam when you bend over for your girl friend's eraser

Flops offers a hilarious yet compassionate approach to a sensitive subject: self-acceptance. Having worked with young people for twelve years, author Fred Hartley effectively tackles this vital area in a clear, relevant manner. He shares successful counseling experiences to demonstrate that these life-changing principles are not just hot air.

We all need to deal with failure — not just the failures we commit — but our failure to bring failures to God. Here Fred Hartley takes us by the hand and leads us through our insecurities, helping us learn to feel good about ourselves. He helps us to see ourselves for who we are and yet be able to say, "Hey, you're pretty good." Fast-paced and vividly illustrated, as well as thoroughly biblical, **Flops** will help us to see that because God never gives up on us, we should never give up on ourselves.

D1114051

BY *Fred Hartley*
UPDATE
DARE TO BE DIFFERENT
GROWING PAINS
100%
FLOPS

Turn your
wipeouts into winners
FLOPS

Fred Hartley

Power Books

Fleming H. Revell Company
Old Tappan, New Jersey

Unless otherwise identified Scripture quotations are from the *Good News Bible*—Old Testament: Copyright © American Bible Society 1976: New Testament: Copyright © American Bible Society 1966, 1971, 1976.

Scripture quotations identified NIV taken from the HOLY BIBLE: NEW INTERNATIONAL VERSION. Copyright © 1973, 1978 by the International Bible Society. Used by permission of Zondervan Bible Publishers.

Scripture quotations identified RSV are from the Revised Standard Version of the Bible, copyrighted 1946, 1952, © 1971 and 1973.

Verses marked TLB are taken from *The Living Bible,* Copyright © 1971 by Tyndale House Publishers, Wheaton, Ill. Used by permission.

Illustrations in this volume are by Gene Haulenbeek.

"In a Little While" by Brown Bannister, Amy Grant, Gary Chapman, and Shane Keister © 1982 by Handrail Music/ASCAP, Addi Music/BMT, Meadowgreen Music Inc. ASCAP and Bug And Bear Music/ASCAP. All rights reserved. International copyright secured. Used by permission.

Quotation from Bill Bright, REVOLUTION NOW, © 1969. Published by Here's Life Publishers. Used by permission.

Library of Congress Cataloging in Publication Data

Hartley, Fred.
  Flops.

  1. Youth—Religious life. 2. Youth—Conduct of life. I. Title.
BV4531.2.H349   1985   248.8'3   85-2336
ISBN 0-8007-5191-4

TO my friends in the
Successful Living family,
who helped convince me
that as a writer I am *not* a flop.

Contents

Turn your
wipeouts into winners
FLOPS

1 Banana Peels

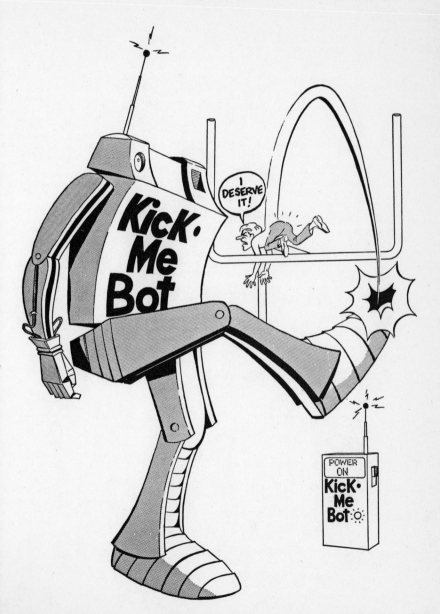

Have you ever felt like a flop?

- Like a joke without a punch line?
- Like a cake that didn't rise?
- Like a painting no one could recognize?
- Like a poem that didn't make any sense?
- Like a tire that went flat?

There are times when we all feel like flops. We have all wrapped our hands around our heads and moaned, "You idiot!"

I'd had my driver's license for only two months, so I was surprised that my dad let me have the car for the evening. I was even more surprised that I was able to get a date with Cathy. She was beautiful. In fact, as far as I was concerned, she was the most beautiful girl in the world— blonde hair, pretty eyes, happy personality, and a cheerleader. Man, I thought I had it made.

I spent most of the afternoon washing and waxing the car. I showered, put on my best clothes, and as I pulled out of the driveway, I can remember feeling really good about myself. The sky was getting darker and darker. By the time I pulled into her driveway, it was raining buckets, but I really didn't care. I was so excited to have a date with her, I would not have cared if bombs were dropping. Her mother loaned us an umbrella, and we strolled arm in arm back to the car. I can remember thinking, *Wow, this couldn't be better.*

I opened the car door, helped her inside, collapsed the umbrella, tossed it in the backseat, and made a mad dash to the other side. I had not noticed the two inches of water that had collected on the grass. When my leather shoes tried to make the turn, it was all over ... *splaaat!* I couldn't believe it! It was as if I was on water skis and had hit a submerged log. I slid five feet more on the seat of my pants. I looked down at my pant legs and couldn't believe my eyes. It looked as though they had been sodded.

By now I was so wet there was no need to hurry, so I made my way to the driver's door, opened it, and slid in, thinking, *You fool! What an idiot!* My only consolation was the fact that I ran around the back of the car so she didn't see me. And it was raining so hard she probably didn't even hear my splash.

All she said when I finally put the key in the ignition was, "Oh, Fred, you're so wet!" I thought to myself, *If you only knew.*

Fortunately, the restaurant where we ate was dimly lit and my pants eventually dried out. I really don't think she ever realized what happened, but I still felt like a jerk. After I dropped her off that evening, and walked back to the scene of the accident, I took a good long look at the rut I had made in the lawn. I hung my head and said, "You are a real jerk! A flop! A nerd! Klutz!" The whole way home in the car that night I saw the splash on instant replay a thousand times. Each time it made me feel like a bigger flop.

Maybe you have never done anything that stupid, but we all have days when we feel like jerks.

Slippery Stepping-stones It can happen so suddenly—we make a mistake, turn on ourselves, and before we know it we are down in the basement, digging holes. We get discouraged, depressed, and soon we become our own worst enemies. It happens to all of us, and it can happen in many different ways.

- Being the first one to sit down in the spelling bee.
- Finding out at the end of the day that you had bad breath.
- Successfully graduating from high school without a single date.
- Wetting the bed, and waking up to realize you are at your friend's house.
- Reading the list for the varsity team and finding your name left out.
- Looking in the mirror Monday morning and finding a big red zit the size of your Adam's apple on your chin.
- Getting introduced by the kid you thought was your best friend, and he forgets your name.
- Having an older sister who is smarter, prettier, and far more popular than you.
- Arriving for a week of camp without toothpaste and underwear.
- Showing up at school in full costume for the masquerade party and finding out it is "next Thursday."
- Panicking when you learn that showers are required for P.E.
- Forgetting your lines in the school play, with your whole family sitting in the front row.

- Ripping your pants out in the seam when you bend over for your girl friend's eraser.

We might as well face the facts: The path of life is paved with slippery stepping-stones. Growing up requires each of us to walk over these stones which are as slippery as banana peels. We all slip and slide, falter and fail, and we will all learn that there are certain things we are good at and there are certain things which we stink at. We can get up in the morning, leave the house, feeling really good about ourselves, and before we know it, we are flat on our backs, feeling like a total flop. We thought our footing was secure but the stepping-stone was too slippery . . . *Splat!*

Quickly, let's look at a few of these slippery stepping-stones.

Banana Peel 1: Our Bodies   You don't need to be a weightlifter or beauty queen to put your body on exhibit. While some bodies get stared at more than others, all bodies are available for public inspection. We get judged for our height and weight, for our complexion, our hair, our breath, the size of our muscles and our curves. Everything needs to be in proper proportion. It's no secret that nice clothes are necessary to make a good impression. We all care what we look like, and we judge ourselves accordingly.

Banana Peel 2: Our Personalities   We are all social creatures. Nobody ever wants to sit alone in the cafeteria. To be treated like a social leper is one disease no kid wants to be caught dead with. It is necessary to break into a small group of friends, and not only to land a date but to be able to land a second and third date, too. We all need friends, and we judge ourselves according to how successful we are at making them and keeping them.

Banana Peel 3: Our Brains Some kids have told me that it is no picnic to be supersmart—that they get teased a lot and called names like "Joe Einstein" or "egghead" or "bookworm." I don't know because I never had that problem. But I can say from experience that being on the bottom of the pile is no fun either. Having your low exam score read aloud to the entire class, flunking a subject and having to take summer school, and stuttering through oral reading are all very threatening. Any one of these is capable of making us feel like idiots. We judge ourselves according to how smart we are.

Banana Peel 4: Our Coordination Most of us have painfully realized that we are not equally good at all sports. That hurts. Some of us have realized that we are not good at *any* sport. That kills. To sit through an awards assembly and never hear your name called over the loudspeaker is a big slap in the face. There is no jacket that is as warm as a varsity jacket, and for those who don't have one, the school year can be long, harsh, cold, and very exposing. We judge ourselves according to our athletic ability.

Banana Peel 5: Our Money To be a teenager you don't have to be a millionaire, but it helps. You need enough money for gas, clothes, records, tapes, clothes, movies, clothes, junk food, video games, concerts, clothes, cosmetics, gum, McDonalds, and enough spending money left over in case anything special comes up. We judge ourselves according to how much money we have, or how much our parents have.

The list of banana peels could include many others—sense of humor, parents, musical talent, and more—but these help make the point.

Now are you ready for this? Here is what happens. You might successfully navigate banana peel numbers 1, 2 and

3, but it only takes one banana peel to bring you down. The critics judge every area, and unless you pass the test scoring 100 percent, you are considered less than normal. It doesn't matter how swift you are on your feet or how much forward momentum you might have or even your leg strength, all it takes is a single banana peel, and it is all over. *Splat. Splash.* Humiliation.

Inferiority I meet teenagers from all over the country. Once we get acquainted and I have earned the right to ask a personal question, I enjoy asking this one: *If you had the power to change anything about yourself, what would it be?*

Even though I have asked the question thousands of times, I am still surprised at the responses, not because the answers are so different, but because they fall within the same predictable areas.

I had only met Sally yesterday on a weekend retreat, but when I asked her the question she said, "How much time do you have to listen?" After a chuckle she added, "Wow! I guess I'd change my looks. I can't stand it—I look just like my mother."

Peter answered the question: "My folks. I wish they didn't get a divorce. It really breaks me up. I'm getting over it now, I guess, but that is one thing I sure would change about my life."

After I got to know Jim he admitted, "I'm not good at nothin'. Everybody else is good at grades or good at a sport or band or somethin'. I wish I was *the best* at somethin' . . . but I'm not the best at nothin'."

I could easily fill an encyclopedia with similar answers, but I think you get the picture. It is a rare bird who feels good about himself all the time. When we don't measure up to our high standards, we fall short and we feel inferior. It's hard to stand up tall when you're stepping on a banana peel.

Down on Ourselves It is easy to get down on ourselves. We can all identify with the cartoon of the guy standing with the contraption he's built—a boot and lever. When he pulls the string, he gets kicked in the rear end. We not only identify with it, there are many times we wished we had such a contraption. To be able to give ourselves a swift kick in the butt would somehow make us feel better—as though we were at least getting what we deserved.

This desire to punish ourselves for our own failures can become a sickness. Here's how it develops.

It starts when we step on our first banana peel, lose our footing, and hit the turf. *Splat!* Humiliated, we get up dizzy, try to regain our equilibrium, only to review the fall in our brains on instant replay dozens of times. Each time we get more and more down on ourselves. After things settle down perhaps we will get up the guts to take another step in that direction only to wipe out again. At this point we move from . . .

- falling to being a *flop*
- feeling ugly to being a *dog*
- losing to being a *loser*
- flunking to being an *idiot*
- feeling cheap to being *worthless*
- rejection to being a *reject*
- being silly to being a *jerk*

Do you notice the difference? The two categories might sound alike, but they are miles apart. The first condemns our ability and that is bad enough, but the second condemns our whole person and that can be devastating. You can be a great guy even though you lose once in a while, but then when you turn on yourself and feel as though losing has become a way of life, you take on the dark identity of being a hardened *loser.* Such a shift is almost like going from life to death.

This book is for everyone who has dropped a pass in the end zone, who has lost a school election, or has forgotten the combination to his locker. If is for those who can't sing solo, can't afford the payments on a car, or can't fall asleep every night without certain regrets.

This book is for all us normal people who at times learn just how normal we are.

When we are down on ourselves, we can't even see ourselves accurately. It is a physical impossibility to see ourselves in the mirror when our heads hang too low. We need to get our chins up at least high enough to take a good look.

It is the purpose of this book to help us all see ourselves for who we are and yet be able to say, "Hey, you're pretty good."

Thoughts

1. What is a "banana peel"?
2. On a scale of 1-10 (10 = perfect; 1 = a total disaster), grade yourself in the following areas:
   a. Your physical appearance _____
   b. Your personality _____
   c. Your brains _____
   d. Your coordination _____
   e. Your finances _____
   f. Your sense of humor _____
3. Have you ever done anything really stupid that made you feel like a nerd? Like building the contraption that would kick you in the butt when you pulled the lever?

   What was it that made you feel that way?

   Why was it such a hard experience?
4. Define "a normal teenager."

   Is he perfect?

   Does he get zits?

   Does he get straight As?
5. What can make a kid feel like a loser?

Feelings

1. What do you like most about yourself? Why?
2. What area(s) of your life make(s) you feel insecure about yourself? Why?
3. If you had the power to change anything about yourself, what would it be? Why did you pick this area? Is it possible to change it?

21

2 When It Hurts to Smile

LOOK AT THE FISH CAUGHT IN THE NET!

GOING HEAD OVER HEELS on a banana peel is bound to draw a crowd. Once we slip and fall on our faces, it doesn't take long until the laughter nearly deafens us. Our generation specializes in making people feel like jerks. There is something that almost makes our mouths water over the slapstick calamity of others. Teenagers can be the world's worst critics, and our friends can become ferocious.

In grammar school, we played kickball every day at recess. As the teams were picked, I was always on one team and Billy on the other because we were the long ball kickers. He and I developed quite a rivalry. One day I was playing outfield, and he blasted a long one. The ball kept going higher and higher, and I kept going back further and further. I was so intent on catching it, I lost all sense of where I was. Smack! My whole body, including the side of my head, flew into the light post. Needless to say, I did not catch the ball. After Billy rounded the bases, he ran out to me, not to offer help or condolences but to help himself to a few cheap laughs. "Wow! Did you see that!" (How could anyone have missed it?) "He looked like a drunk! Ha! Ha! Ha!" He laughed so hard he almost split his sides. As I recall, just about everyone else chimed in with a chuckle too. That laughter only made me feel worse.

A few weeks later he blasted another one over my head. He thought he had an easy home run. I grabbed the ball on the first bounce, ran it in as fast as I could and tossed it at him as he was rounding third base. It was such a long shot, he wasn't even looking. By chance, it caught him between

25

the legs. He didn't know what hit him and slid halfway to home. He not only tore a giant hole in his pants, but he looked like a beached whale. I confess that I enjoyed every minute of it.

We can all identify with this animal instinct that makes us drool with delight over the misery of others.

Obviously Have you ever noticed that most joking and mocking takes the obvious and makes it *painfully* obvious?

- You strike out in the bottom of the ninth inning and your best friend moans, "You fanned! You were our last hope and you blew it." (You feel like saying, "I know, I know.")
- You go to class with a few painfully ripe pimples and some kid says, "Good grief! Have you looked in the mirror this morning? Disgusting!" (You feel like saying, "Hey, I've been looking at them since five-thirty this morning.")
- Your friend says over the phone, "I can't believe you didn't get invited to Sally's party Friday night. I thought *everybody* got invited." (You feel like saying, "Hey, I already feel like I've got social sleeping sickness, you don't have to rub it in.")
- You slip in the lunchroom, and your tray goes flying and half the student body screams, "Klutz!" "Idiot," "Spaz," "Gorilla Fingers," "Fool." When the names stop, they break out into wild applause, then laughter, and you don't know what to say.

In each case, the mocking restates the obvious. Friends and enemies join together to stick a magnifying glass under our noses to help us see what was already in full view—as if we didn't know we had struck out, as if we weren't already painfully aware that the candy bars we ate over the weekend plastered zits all over our faces, or as if we intentionally threw food in the cafeteria.

A Flop by Any Name There are all different kinds of names given to "flops." Depending on what part of the country you are from, you will use one or more or a combination of several of the following.

For those with *personality* problems:
Nerd, Fish, Jerk, Fruitcake, Pansy, Maggot, Roach, Toad, Worm, Zero, Weirdo, Turkey, Wallflower, Rodent, Hot Dog, Loser.

For those with *intellectual* problems:
Imbecile, Fool, Idiot, Raca, Pea Brain, Air Head, Space Cadet, Stupid, Meathead, Moron, Fuzzball, Retard, Mastodon.

For those with *physical* problems:
Dog, Saddlebags, Blimp, Toad, Pretzel, Crater Face, Moss Mouth, Fire Hydrant, Metal Mouth, Shrimp, Tinsel Teeth, Ox, Moose, Q-tip, Dandelion, Scab.

For those with *agility* problems:
Klutz, Jerk, Hop-along, Spaz.

For those *with moral principles:*
Mama's Boy, Jesus Freak, Goody-Goody, Prude, Cream Puff, Cornball, Square, Joe Christian, Powder Puff.

For those *without moral principles:*
Slut, Whore, Playboy, Wolf, Fag, Creep.

Essentially, all these names do the same thing; they take the obvious and make it painfully obvious. They also make many people hate themselves.

Hooks With Barbs It doesn't take long until we begin believing what we hear. "After all," we say to ourselves, "that many people can't be wrong." If you hear words like *ugly, klutz, idiot* often enough, you will start using them to refer to yourself.

Harsh names like these go in much easier than they come out. We can casually call another kid a nasty name. It slips out so easily, we might not even mean much by it. We knew it would bring a sure laugh, and we figured someone else would have said it anyway, so what difference did it make? Little did we realize the effect that word would have on the other person, especially when the other person happened to be our best friend. The word that slipped out so easily got stuck in the other person's heart, and that poor person is having a miserable time getting it out.

Have you ever gotten a fishhook in your hand? It goes in like a simple straight pin, but getting it out is always a mess. With a barb on the hook you have only four unpleasant options: pull it out and lose a good chunk of flesh with it, take hook and finger to the doctor and let him cut it out, push it clear through to the other side, or leave it. In the same way, being called a name that hurts slips under the surface easily, gets lodged inside, and the more you play with it or pull against it, the more painful it gets.

Explanations and apologies sound hollow to those hurt by our jesting. It is not easy to forgive when you are the one left with barbed hooks in your heart. Nevertheless, an apology usually sounds like this, "Hey, c'mon, don't take it so hard. We're still friends aren't we? You know I was only kidding. Hey, I admit it was a silly thing to say, but I was getting embarrassed. . . . I mean, you and I do spend a lot of time together and I didn't want them thinking that we agree on everything. . . . I mean, everybody needs to be able to take a joke. You must admit, it was pretty funny." Somehow words don't work. No matter how sorry we are, apologies don't remove fishhooks.

We all assume we will have a few enemies whose attacks we are prepared to handle. But when a *friend* attacks, the barriers are usually down, and the effect can be devastating. It is one thing to be excluded from the enemy camp; that's to be expected. But when we get excluded from our own camp, it's like getting thrown out in a blizzard naked.

"I Thought You Were My Friend" Have you ever wondered why when you flopped, it was usually your friends who led the laughter? Why they were the first ones to call you the name, crack the joke, state the obvious? It is usually a matter of reputation. Many times after a kid gets mocked I have seen him look at his buddy who just threw the verbal pie in his face as if to say, "How could you? I thought you were my friend." Then, the friend looks back with halfway sorry eyes as if to say, "Hey, c'mon, don't you understand? I had to protect myself."

A few kids ended up at the soda shop after school. A couple of guys slid quickly into the booth next to a cute cheerleader. When the overweight girl slid in across the table, the guys remaining looked at each other, hesitating just long enough to preserve their reputation. They had shown that the girl was not their choice. Not a word was said, but everyone got the message, especially the girl. How many times does that need to happen until she feels like a leftover?

Your friend is not as physically developed as most in the class. You already know that because you often spend the night at each other's houses, but today in the locker room when her figure becomes the object of humor, you jump right in. Others jest, "Yeah, you pancake . . . ironing board . . . ha, ha, ha." But you dare to ask, "Are you sure you are a girl?" Others laughed when you said it, but as you look at her face, you wish you hadn't said a word. Later, when the two of you are alone, you apologize but you know that it is not the same, and it probably won't be for a few days.

Mocking others is actually a sign of our insecurity. Weak, handicapped people make insecure people feel even more insecure. However, as we begin to accept ourselves for who we are, accepting others comes a lot easier. In fact, once we accept ourselves, we can help others accept themselves, too. Real friends don't mock.

Gnats, Vultures, and Sharks Friends can be like gnats. Every spring I play softball, and in some games before the end of the season I am sure to get a "raspberry" on my knee or upper thigh. (A raspberry is an area of skin that has been rubbed raw.) You see, my favorite part of the game is base running, so I usually do a fair amount of sliding. When you first notice the raspberry, it is not red but rather black—covered with gnats. These little bugs enjoy the taste of white blood cells and quickly take advantage of the exposed area. Do the gnats remind you of this same tendency in yourself? If we see someone fall and skin his knee, like gnats, we instinctively relish landing on his exposed area and sucking on it for all it's worth.

Friends can be like vultures. Not long ago, I was reading a book under a large tree, and I fell asleep. When I awoke, it was almost frightening to see several large vultures overlooking me. When they noticed I was not dead, they flew off disappointed. They had hoped to make a meal out of me if only my bones were covered with rotting flesh. Do the vultures remind you of this same tendency in yourself? When we come to the scene of an accident, we sit there licking our chops, waiting to see blood.

Friends can be like sharks. Living in south Florida, I enjoy fishing. Off Sanibel Island, I enjoy shark fishing. Here's how it works: You take a live fish, insert a large hook through its body, and toss it out. Usually, it doesn't take long to get some action. The first shark I ever saw was swimming around my bait for twenty minutes. Finally, I pulled in my line, cut a hole in the stomach of my bait fish (not large enough to kill it, just large enough to let it bleed), and tossed it back. Within minutes, the shark mouthed, chewed, and swallowed it. The rest of the action was mine. He was a fine lemon shark that I landed, cleaned, and cooked. (Yes, you can eat shark.) Does the shark remind you of the same tendency in yourself? As disgusting as this sounds, we can go wild and attack those who are wounded, bleeding, or handicapped.

To kick a man when he is down or even to laugh may come naturally, but it is animalistic and beastly. We are not insects, birds, or fish. We are man, and as man we are created in God's own image, and as we pick away at an exposed area, or feed off someone else's accident, we are attacking not just man but God.

Soon after I met Jesus and turned my life over to Him, I was invited to a picnic with a bunch of other Christians. The tallest, thinnest girl I had ever seen walked past our table. Several heads turned and smiled but I cracked the joke. One of the girls in our group, a far more mature Christian than I, lovingly and immediately corrected, "God loves her as much as He loves you." The truth of that statement knocked the wind out of me. I was caught acting like an animal again even though Jesus had treated me so much better than an animal.

When It Hurts to Smile After we fall and maybe get kicked while we're down, we eventually get back up and pretend that it didn't hurt. We know that it helps if we laugh at ourselves, but sometimes that is hard when we are crying inside. Somehow there is no pain quite as severe as the pain you keep to yourself.

There are times you just wish you could excuse yourself from high school and go hibernate. Sometimes you just feel totally out of place, like there is nowhere you belong. You feel about as out of place as the time I walked into a public rest room, closed the stall door only to notice the feet of the person next to me—nylons with high heels! (QUESTION: How does a man graciously excuse himself from a ladies' room at a fashionable restaurant? ANSWER: Very quickly!) I assure you, that was a very embarrassing moment, but it was not nearly as bad as some of the awkward experiences kids have every day in high school. In high school there are few places to hide.

Thoughts

1. Why do we naturally laugh when others fall on their faces or goof up? Why do accidents draw a crowd?
2. We have all heard the saying, "Sticks and stones can break my bones, but names will never hurt me." Is it really true? Respond.
3. Why are *friends* often the ones who mock the loudest?
4. Why does it hurt the most when friends attack?
5. Why are gnats, vultures, and sharks included in this chapter?
6. Define *jealousy*. What is the difference between jealousy and competition? How is jealousy involved in criticizing others?
7. Define *prejudice*. Besides racial, what other prejudices are common?
8. Why do we compare ourselves to each other? Is it healthy?
9. How should we respond to people who are different from us? To people with handicaps?

Feelings

1. Have you ever been called an unflattering name? How did it make you feel?
2. Have you ever been really embarrassed? So embarrassed that it hurt? So hurt that you cried? What exactly happened? Why did it hurt so badly?
3. Have you ever felt like staying home from school just to avoid your friends? Describe the feeling. What causes it?
4. Have you ever felt jealous? Describe the feeling. How did it show itself? What did you do about it?

33

3 Mirror, Mirror; Which Mirror?

I BRAKE FOR TOADS

ZIT ZAP

AMUSEMENT PARKS and carnivals usually have curved mirrors which are good for a few grins. As you stand in front of some of them, they make you appear short and stubby, with legs that look like they were sawed off at the knees. Take a step back, and you shoot up to be a tall man on stilts. As you stand in front of another mirror, you look like a skinny bean pole, and then by taking a half-step to the side, you turn into Porky Pig. Mirrors always give us a reflection of who we are, but they are not always accurate. Sometimes they give us a distorted perspective.

The way we look at ourselves depends on where we see our reflection. It is a physical impossibility to see ourselves face-to-face without using some sort of mirror, so if the mirror is no good, we will never get a true picture of who we are.

Messed-Up Mirrors   Looking at the wrong mirror can make any of us feel ugly . . . like freaks in a circus. We need to be careful which mirrors we are standing in front of when we ask the question, "Who am I?" Let's consider a few messed-up mirrors with which we are all familiar.

• **The Too-Tall Mirror**   There is an unrealistically high standard by which we have all judged ourselves. It is called *perfection*, and you don't need to be a perfectionist to stand in front of it.

We have seen enough beauty pageants, Hollywood stars, and cover-girl smiles to have ingrained on our brains that in

37

order to be normal, you need to have a mouth full of teeth that glisten like moist Chiclets, eyes the size of a basset hound's, and a complexion as smooth as a baby's belly. Those sexy ones who shoot carefree down Colorado rapids, sipping Cokes, skydive hand in hand, or skin-dive in shoelace bikinis have painted a picture of the good life. Unfortunately, this picture sits on top of the average kid and crushes him until he cries, "uncle." Most of us have come to the conclusion there is no way we can compete against such odds. Darwin's principle of survival of the fittest is all too true in most high schools; it has made many a teen feel like a monkey.

Let me tell you something:

- Nobody has perfect teeth unless they have all been ripped out and replaced with plastic.
- If you look close enough, even the beauty queens have warts, somewhere.
- Some of the cover girls are the most insecure people in the world.
- No one scores a perfect 10.

The mirror that makes us feel ugly because our nose is a little bumpy, or because our hair is unmanageable, or because we can't even make a lay-up needs to be smashed. We each need to admit we have looked too often into the too-tall mirror and that it has made us feel too small. It sets an unrealistically high standard that is virtually unattainable. While we are not all perfectionists, we have all compared ourselves (perhaps even unknowingly) with perfection, and found ourselves coming up short. We need to understand that this does not mean that there is anything wrong with us. All it means is we have been looking into the wrong mirror. It is unfair to compare ourselves against some image of perfection that is way over our heads.

• *Somebody Else's Mirror*   It is so easy to fall into the trap of trying to see yourself in someone else's mirror. Here's how it works.

Someone special starts getting our attention. We focus long enough on him, and he becomes a hero, a giant, an idol—someone we not only look up to, but someone we worship and someone we want to be.

Musicians, movie stars, models, songwriters, rock stars have all become teenage idols. Kids dress like them, walk like them, cut their hair like them, dance like them, all because they want to *be* like them.

Professional athletes have the same appeal. Kids want to swing the bat like Reggie Jackson, release the football like Dan Marino, prance around the ring like Marvin Hagler, and stroke the racquet like Chris Evert Lloyd.

We have all heard of Michaelmania . . . the disease that had thousands of kids wishing they were Michael Jackson. More than simply breaking all records for album and video sales, hero worship hit an all-time high. In every city across the country there are little Jackson look-alikes with the typical Sergeant Pepper's jacket and single white, sequined glove. Fads are fads, but they get bad when they go too far. Outside of one live concert, a fan-atic said, "I'm getting an operation in December"—plastic surgery to look more like his hero, Michael Jackson. He explained that his parents were allowing it because "I showed my mother the story of the guy in England who committed suicide because his parents wouldn't get him an operation." That is a classic example of a fad going too far. That fad is sad—even bad!

This same tendency can be seen on the local school level, too. The kid in your class who has no problem getting dates, setting the trends, cracking the jokes, and making the moves always gets imitated. People start using the same expressions, wearing the same style shoes, whistling the same tunes, and breaking the same rules. If the girl is a marijuana smoker, those who follow her lead will all smoke marijuana. If the guy swears, his little following will also learn to swear. Usually what we admire about such a person initially is their influence, and as we follow his lead, we give him even greater influence.

While it is perfectly natural for everyone to have a hero, we were never intended to find out who we are by looking into someone else's mirror. In fact, this can be highly destructive.

What happens when the guy five foot six envies a guy six foot three? (He feels like a runt.)

Or what happens when an eleventh-grade water boy idolizes the tenth-grade starting quarterback? (He feels like a drip.)

Or what happens when the girl whose younger sister gets asked to the senior prom stays home and watches the clock? (She feels like an old maid.)

Do you know what happens when we look into somebody else's mirror? We never find out who we really are. All we discover is who we are not, and that's depressing. When it comes to finding out who we really are, we need to smash all the mirrors meant for other people because they put an unrealistic burden on us and keep us from ever discovering our own personal uniqueness. It is one thing to admire certain qualities about another person, but the trouble starts when we want to *be* them. When we would rather be someone else, we are guilty of idolatry, and idolatry is sin. It is a sin against the creativity of God and against yourself, His creation.

If you have been trying to copy someone else, you might as well knock it off. The only person you will ever be is the one God intended you to be, and you will never discover who that special person is by looking into someone else's mirror.

• *The Distorted Mirror*   The other day I was in a rush to get ready for a dinner appointment, and I needed to shave. Ordinarily I never shave while my wife is showering because the whole bathroom looks like a steam bath—I can hardly see through the fog, and condensation covers the mirror. It happened that my wife was in the shower, but I didn't have time to let that slow me down. I lathered up, grabbed my razor, and started stroking. Incredible! By the time I was done and the fog had lifted, I saw that I had nicked myself so badly, I was lucky to have a nose left. I should have left the whiskers; at least they looked better than the scabs.

What was the problem? Don't I know how to shave? Sure I know how to shave, but the mirror was messed up, distorted. Distorted mirrors can get us in a great deal of trouble. They can almost convince us that we need to cut off our noses to get even with our ugly faces.

I knew a kid, Howard, who thought he was stupid because his second-grade teacher treated him like a moron. One day she even called him "Dummy" which his classmates were quick to pick up on and the nickname stuck. It didn't take him long until he started using "Dummy" to refer to himself. When he walked into fifth grade, he waved at his teacher, smiled and said, "Hi, I am Howard the Dummy." His teacher confronted him, "No, you're not, and I don't ever want to hear you say that again." That year she taught him that he was not stupid. She gave him positive feedback that made him feel good about himself. Today Howard is a professor at a leading graduate school. In a sense we could say, she helped Howard smash the distorted mirror that kept him from seeing who he really was.

I have known a number of kids who are convinced that they are ugly. When I ask, "Why?" They say, "Aw, man, everyone knows I'm nothing to look at." I try to pursue it, "Well, who exactly told you so?" They usually end up admitting something like this: "No one ever told me; I just don't like the way they treat me." Unfortunately, public opinion is not a good mirror in which to accurately see ourselves, and yet it is one of the most popular.

Many have already come to the conclusion that they stink at sports, but the only reason they give is, "I tried out for freshman football and quit," or "When I was a kid, my dad told me I couldn't even swing the bat." A single encounter with a banana peel should not keep us from walking again, and yet it often does. We get negative feedback from a coach, a parent, a friend, the team, and we jump to the conclusion we are uncoordinated klutzes.

The problem is negative criticism does not give us a fair view of ourselves because it is always only partial—it doesn't take in the whole picture, only the weak side. Yet when we get criticized, and usually too harshly, all we focus on is the negative and that hurts.

• *No Mirror (lessons from a monster movie)*   As a

teenager I used to love the Friday-night monster movies. One of my favorites was about a mad scientist whose wife was badly burned as an experiment backfired in his laboratory. She didn't get singed; she was char-broiled, and the flesh on her face was like a giant scab. To be nice to everyone else, he insisted she wear gauze bandages on her face, and to be nice to her, he ordered all the mirrors smashed on the island on which they lived. At least then no one would have to look at her, and she would not be able to look at herself. He was afraid she might flip her lid if she found out what she really looked like.

He thought he was protecting her; however, as a result, she resented him and hated herself. She knew that if she was so ugly that her own husband would hide her from herself, her face must have been brutal.

As you might expect, eventually the hero of the story risks his life to bring her a mirror. She braces herself, takes off the gauze cloth, looks into the mirror, and to everyone's amazement, she survives the shock. She was not pretty. In fact, her skin looked like a baked potato, but at least the suspense was over, the big question was answered, and her curiosity was satisfied. She was even able to accept herself.

This story is certainly crude, but it illustrates where a pile of teenagers are at. There are many who spend a great volume of energy running away from themselves. They are afraid to see themselves face to face. They hate the mirror. They have chosen to run and hide. Hey, sometimes as we lie in bed, thinking about ourselves and some of the stupid things we said and did during the day, we might think we are watching a horror film. There are times when we wish we could hijack the space shuttle just to avoid having to show up at class the next day.

Trying to answer the question, "Who am I?" by looking into messed-up mirrors will not work, but looking into no mirror is not much of an alternative. You can play hide-and-seek all by yourself for a little while, but then it gets boring. When you run out of places to hide, the game is over. We can never get away from ourselves.

The True Mirror The six-million-dollar question is this: *Where do I look to find out who I am?* And another question equally as important: *Who will tell me if I am OK?*

There is only one Person who can tell you if you are okay and that is your Creator, and the place to discover who you are is in the mirror of His Book, the Bible. Who can tell if an automobile is operating at full efficiency better than the man who designed and built it? Who knows what the poem is supposed to be communicating better than the person who wrote it? Who can tell you about yourself better than God who made you and loves you? And unlike the automobile, when God created you, He put a patent on you that He will never use again. You are unique. When you look in the mirror of His Book, you get an honest, straightforward view of who you are. God is not a mad scientist who allows experiments to blow up in our faces. Nor does He hide us from seeing who we really are. He loves us enough to let us see ourselves, and He helps us accept ourselves, too.

A Living Example This whole idea that God can show us who we are and then help us accept ourselves might sound like a pile of bologna—just a lot of fat words. Let me put some muscle behind it. Stephen is his name. Stephen, a high-school senior was in my office today and told me that for the past six years he had lived in a fantasy world. He had no friends, no hobbies, no fun. He never talked to anyone, including his parents. He'd come home from school, shut his door, play rock-and-roll music, and smoke pot. As he began to feel more comfortable talking with me, he admitted, "I was a jerk. I didn't want to open up to anyone because I didn't know how and I didn't think anyone would like me anyway. I was a real loner." When I asked him, "What did you think about yourself?" he responded, "Not much. I tried not to think about it." In a sense he was living in a world without mirrors.

Fortunately, there is a change taking place in Stephen's life. I asked him, "Right now, who or what makes you feel good about yourself?"

He answered with one word, "God." Then he explained, "God designed me. By reading the Bible, I have really come to understand that God loves me and that I can't be a zero because I'm special to Him." At first I thought he might have been feeding me answers a minister would like to hear, but I don't think so any longer. He went on, "God is teaching me to face myself. I don't have to play mind games anymore. He's teaching me who I am, and He's teaching me that I'm okay. I can talk to people now. I'm not off on an island all by myself. I can reach out and talk to people because I'm not afraid of them and what they will think of me." Pretty good, huh?

If you are afraid to face yourself, afraid that you might not be able to stomach the sight, you have probably gotten a distorted glimpse of yourself. If you don't like the looks of yourself, one thing is for sure, the look you took was not in the Book, because the Book is honest and kind. It might be the hardest thing in the world to get you to take another look, but I am going to try.

Thoughts

1. "Darwin's principle of survival of the fittest is all too true in most high schools; it has made many a teen feel like a monkey." Respond.
2. Mirrors determine the way we see ourselves. List some characteristics of the following mirrors.
   a. Too-tall mirror
   b. Somebody else's mirror
   c. Distorted mirror
   d. No mirror
3. Which is the most common mirror that gives most kids a distorted view of themselves?
4. What are some of the negative effects of getting a distorted view of ourselves?
5. Why is it important to have an accurate view of who we are?
6. Do you know anyone like Stephen (no friends, no hobbies, no fun, no one to talk to)?
7. What difference did God make in Stephen's life?
8. "If you don't like the looks of yourself, one thing is for sure, the look you took is not in the Book, because the Book is honest and kind." Discuss.

Feelings

1. Have you ever felt lonely—as though no one really knew who you were? Use seven different words to describe the feeling.
2. Stephen's life changed when he saw himself from God's perspective. How would your feelings about yourself change if you understand you are God's special creation?

4 A Matter of Life and Death

YEAH... THE GREATEST FLOP!

LET ME ASK *you* the same question I asked Stephen: *Right now, who or what makes you feel good about yourself?* We all need somebody or something telling us we are okay. It is actually a matter of life and death.

David was a happy-go-lucky freckle-faced nine-year-old when his father, Robert F. Kennedy, was nominated to run for the United States Senate in New York. When his dad was elected, he became more and more his hero. Three years later things really got exciting when RFK ran in the presidential primary. Twelve-year-old David saw in his father everything he wanted to be and more. When they couldn't travel together, David watched all the newscasts to catch a glimpse of his hero.

On the night of June 5, 1968, instead of being asleep as he should have been, he decided to watch his dad give his victory speech after winning the California primary. The TV moment was filled with excitement and Kennedy charisma, and all the campaign workers were obviously eating it up. As RFK turned from the podium and made his way to an adjoining room, suddenly the applause turned to screams of horror. People panicked. Television cameras lunged wildly. Voices burst like bullets. Then came the picture that brought the nation to its knees ... Robert Kennedy lying face down in the red puddle of his own blood. I can remember as a teenager watching it and weeping. What I and millions of Americans did not realize was that David Kennedy, Robert's son, was sitting in a Los Angeles hotel room watching it all with us.

Biographer Theodore H. White discovered young David in the room hours later still watching the newscasts—replay after replay. That night—and for years afterwards—David saw his dad die; and more than his dad, he lost an enormous chunk of who he was. He was a Kennedy, specifically, the senator's son. But now he was the *late* senator's son and that was devastating. Beyond the normal grief over such a loss, David faced an enormous identity crisis. His dad, his hero, his ideal, his model man had been destroyed right before his eyes, and he would never fully get over it.

From that breaking point things began to fall apart in David's life. He started smoking marijuana early in his teens and moved on to harder drugs in prep school. After three years of Harvard, he quit and hung out at Studio 54 and Xenon, nightclubs in New York City. He was arrested in Virginia for doing ninety-two mph without a driver's license or vehicle registration. The list of fragments could go on and on.

Those at a distance might ask, "How could a kid from such fine stock do such nasty things?" But some who were closer to him would answer, "Fine stock didn't do him any good once he was uprooted and his heart was broken." He was almost like a tree trying to grow on a concrete expressway divider. He had nowhere to send down roots.

Although reports were conflicting, David spent the last few days of life in despair—bouncing from bar to bar, snorting cocaine through a twenty-dollar bill, drinking vodka at poolside, and weeping to an unknown woman about all the pain he felt since seeing his father shot to death on television. "I never find peace inside," he said. "I've been full of pain . . . I am crying for help."

Wednesday, April 25, 1984, his body was found draped between two mattresses at the Brazilian Court Hotel in Palm Beach. The medical examiner's office determined to that considerable alcohol and narcotics had passed through his bloodstream, but David's death was not ruled a suicide. It didn't need to be. It seemed obvious to some that he didn't want to live anyway.

Harrison Raine, author of *Growing Up Kennedy: The Third Wave Comes of Age,* was reported to have said, "He was the one that was the most devastated by the death of his father . . . he was the one that reacted the most destructively to his pain" (*Miami Herald,* April 26, 1984). Others agreed, "If his father's death hit David harder than the others, it was because there had been a special bond between them—both were the runts of the litter, sandwiched into the middle of a large family" (Peter Collier, and David Horowitz, *Young Kennedys: The Decline of an American Dynasty*).

The official five-hundred-page report on young Kennedy's death revealed that his body contained a fatal mixture of four ingredients: vodka, cocaine, a tranquilizer and a painkiller. Tragically, Kennedy spent the last sixteen years of his life reaching for painkillers that did not work.

The last Sunday he lived was Easter Sunday. He got "the shakes" and sent for a fresh supply of cocaine. He also sent for a priest who held Mass in David's room at 1:00 P.M. for him and a few friends. The priest was unsuccessful at giving David lasting relief.

Why Suicide? The big question surrounding such an untimely death is "why?" "Why would a guy raised in such a fine family with so much going for him want to take his own life?"

Have you ever known anyone who attempted suicide? Have you ever thought of it yourself?

The fact is, 7,000 teenagers kill themselves every year, and an estimated 400,000 make an attempt at it. A psychologist in California estimates that over 1 million teenagers a year consider it. This marks a 300 percent increase over the past two decades. We think the murder rate is bad, but actually more people kill themselves than kill others. In Chicago, the suicide hotline rings every twenty seconds. Today there are even books available that list 1,001 ways to take your own life. (Let it be noted that such books have been unable to get endorsements from satisfied customers.)

There are many reasons why people choose to put an end to themselves, but mingled with all the others is usually this single common thread: *a shattered self-image.* Once we move from failing to being a *failure,* or from feeling cheap to being *worthless,* we have reached a danger zone. If we ever lose the sense of our own self-worth, it won't take long until we lose the will to go on living. For this reason we can say, the way we feel about ourselves is a matter of life and death.

It goes sort of like this: "I hurt inside, no one to talk with. No one understands me. No one really cares. No one tells me that I'm okay . . . at least no one who really matters. I guess I'm not worth much anyway. So, why not do away with myself?" Usually prior to attempted suicide there are dozens of appeals for attention, in a sense begging, "Hey, won't somebody out there tell me I'm okay . . . that I'm worth something?" Often the attempted suicide is in itself a final desperate cry for affirmation of self-worth:

"I wonder if anyone will cry at my funeral? Will they even notice that I'm gone?"

Big Enough? Let me ask you the question again, "Right now, who or what makes you feel good about yourself?"

- It might be your coach patting you on the back for your great potential.
- It might be your dad treating you like his favorite.
- It might be your boyfriend or girl friend who wants to be with you more than anyone else in the world.

Let me ask you another question, "Whatever it is that makes you feel good about yourself, is it big enough?"

Your coach might think you are the greatest baseball player since Mickey Mantle but is he big enough? Donny thought so. But then he lost his leg in a car accident, and was no longer able to play ball. Before the accident he was a baseball player and a good one. After the accident he was no longer an athlete, so who was he? He felt like a nobody. His coach never came to see him in the hospital; he never even sent a card.

What do you do when your boyfriend breaks up with you or you see him looking longingly at the new girl in class? Suddenly you feel like a leftover, a reject, a nobody. You feel put down, betrayed, hurt. This past year in North Salem, New York, a high-school couple quarreled. The girl, last year's homecoming queen, went out and killed herself. Within three weeks her boyfriend hanged himself with his belt in the bathroom of his own home. This case hit the papers, but it is not unique. Every week in every school teenagers are devastated by breaking up. When the person who made your life worthwhile is no longer there to hold you and kiss you and make you feel special, it doesn't take much to come to the conclusion that life is *not* worthwhile anymore. Even a boyfriend or girl friend is not big enough to answer the question, "Am I okay?"

David Kennedy saw himself in his father. His father was almost a superhero—bigger than life. He made David feel good about himself. Any boy certainly would have idolized his dad as David did. The problem was even David's dad was not big enough. He was snatched by the assassin's bullet, and David was left with nothing but an empty shell. The broken dreams and unfulfilled expectations left David devastated. From then on no one adequately answered the questions, "Who am I?" and "Am I okay?"

Things Are Definitely Too Small   When *people* stop clapping, we can look to *things* to make us feel good about ourselves: new stylish clothes, winning a trophy with our name engraved, sophisticated stereo equipment to blast us out, a flashy new car, drugs.

Things can be fun, but they are not big enough to make us feel special. If we feel good about ourselves because of some material objects, what will happen when those things break down? When my car gets totaled or when my trophy gets tarnished? I'll go to pieces. People who base their self-esteem on material objects are some of the most insecure people you will ever meet.

From Death to Life   Who then is big enough to make me feel good about myself? The only One big enough to make me feel good about myself is God. His feelings toward me are not fickle. He won't reject me to fall in love with someone else. He won't get in an accident or run out of gas. He will never fall to an assassin's bullet. He isn't going to get tarnished or lose His luster. If something ever happens to me, He certainly makes hospital visits, and no one can ever take Him away from me. In fact, when you first see yourself from God's perspective and understand how much He cares, it is almost like getting raised from the dead.

All her life Sandy felt like a loser. Even though she was the youngest child, she never felt special. She was no dog, but she'd never win a beauty contest. She wasn't stupid, but she studied hard and still never made honor roll. She went to church to keep her parents happy, but she never got much out of it. When the boy down the street started showing an interest in her, she started to blossom. She talked more, smiled more, did things around the house. She felt more important and wanted to contribute.

When the boy wanted to take some of her clothes off, at first she felt guilty, but quickly rationalized, "Why not? He loves me . . . he makes me feel so special." It didn't take long until it happened every day after school, as long as her mother wasn't home. As far as Sandy was concerned, it was a beautiful little fantasy just between the two of them.

The phone rang. It was Gina, the girl next door. "So I hear you and Mark are doing your thing together," she snickered. Sandy's silence gave her away, so Gina continued, "Aw, c'mon, you don't have to hide it from me. Mark used to come over to my house every day, too. I know all about it. He tells you it's the first time. He says there's nothing wrong with it. He makes you feel like a nerd if you don't, so you go along with it." Still there was no answer. Sandy felt exposed, betrayed, taken. "Hey, go ahead, enjoy it while it lasts. Before me, it was Laura, and after you, it will be someone else. Well, have a nice afternoon." *Click.*

Those few words cut so deep into Sandy's heart, she felt as if she had drunk a thermos of battery acid. She was being eaten alive inside. Nowhere she could go, nothing she could do could get it out of her mind. Her thoughts raced, "But he's the only one who's ever loved me. . . . I said I never would until I got married. . . . Gina's just jealous. . . . I'm going to ask him; surely he'll tell me it's not true. . . . All he wanted me to be was a little plaything . . . I'm a cheap, two-bit idiot. . . . I don't ever want to see him again."

That afternoon, rather than facing Mark, she took a prescription bottle from the medicine cabinet, hopped on her bike, and headed for a vacant lot where she used to play. As she chewed the pills one by one, she could hear the nails hammering into her coffin. As her mind buzzed and body got numb, she panicked. "Hey, I don't want to die. This is stupid. What am I doing?" But it was too late. She was too dizzy to ride her bike or even walk. She was too weak to call out for help. But she wasn't too weak to pray, "Oh, God, help me. Please help! This was stupid, God. I'm sorry. Somehow, get me out of this one, please!"

Several hours later she woke up in the hospital, looking up into the face of her mother. She cried. They both cried and hugged and said they were sorry. Fortunately, Sandy's mom came home early from work, sensed something was wrong when the medicine-cabinet door was open and her bike was gone. After checking with a few neighbors, she looked at the only other place she could think of.

That evening Sandy's pastor visited her in the hospital. They talked together about how Sandy felt toward herself. She admitted that she felt like a fool. Needless to say, she was ready to listen to someone. Rather than condemning her, the man assured her that God loved her and that she was special to Him. He read Psalm 139 to her and asked her to read it every day for a month which she did. In fact, she memorized it word for word. By seeing herself in God's Word from God's perspective, she understood that she was special, because she was special to God. She learned that God made her as a unique creation and that her looks and abilities and family were all according to God's wonderful design.

When I met her at camp two years later and she explained all this to me, I saw a person who had truly been born again. "Jesus Christ not only forgave me of my sins," she explained, "but when I accepted Him as my Saviour, I was able to accept myself. I not only fell in love with my Lord, but I received a healthy love for myself." When I asked her what changes she's seen in her life since then, her face lit up. "You wouldn't believe it. First of all, my parents and I do stuff together now. I have really come to appreciate them. I really don't think they've changed, but I have. At school I've gotten a lot more involved with projects and clubs. I'm really not any better at it, I just have more fun. And since I've come to accept myself, other people seem to like me better, too—at least I have a lot more friends. As far as guys are concerned, I still don't date that much, but for now it's probably better that way. At least I don't feel like I need to be a slut in order to get a guy to like me anymore. And then, between me and God ... well, it's like everything is new. I used to know *about* Jesus, but now I really know *Him.* Before I'd almost resent Him because I didn't like the person He made me, but now I think He's great. I still goof up once in a while, but I know He loves me, accepts me, and welcomes me back. Isn't it wild that God did all that for me?"

The reason God is able to do all that is because He is big enough. He is bigger than we are, and He is able to make us feel good about ourselves in a way no one else is able.

Thoughts

What events contributed to the destruction of David Kennedy's life? Have you ever known anyone like him? Has anything happened in your life that lets you in some way identify with him?

2. List some reasons so many kids consider suicide.
3. Who or what makes most people feel good about themselves?
4. How can we get hurt and lose respect for ourselves while dating?
5. When Sandy dated the neighbor boy, what was she looking for?
6. When she was in the hospital, what change occurred in her life? Years later, what were the results?
7. Why is this chapter entitled "A Matter of Life and Death"? Specifically, what is "a matter of life and death"?

Feelings

1. Be honest . . . right now, who or what makes you feel good about yourself?
2. When you are lonely—really lonely—what do you do? Where do you go? What do you think about?
3. Have you ever hurt so badly that you cried? What caused the pain?
4. Even if you never believed in God before, describe what it would do to you if you discovered that He loved you personally, that He not only created you, but that He wants to be your friend.

58

5 A Look in the Book

GOD IS ABLE to show us who we are, and He helps us accept ourselves. The question is, do you have the guts to look in His mirror? Some people are afraid they might not like what they see. Even though I have not met you, I assure you that when you see yourself the way God sees you, you will be thrilled at the discovery.

When my son was less than a year old he crawled up to a mirror, took one look at himself and went bananas! He smiled, chuckled out loud, pushed on the mirror, pinched his cheeks, licked the mirror, and made plenty of faces. He literally drooled over himself. It was a brand-new experience, and he couldn't get enough of it. Similarly, it is a liberating experience for God to show us who we really are. It might be a little extreme if we started drooling over ourselves, but there is nothing wrong with having a healthy appreciation. After all, we are God's creation.

Did you know that the Bible calls itself a mirror?

. . . So don't fool yourselves. For if a person just listens and doesn't obey, he is like a man looking at his face in a mirror; as soon as he walks away, he can't see himself anymore or remember what he looks like. But if anyone keeps looking steadily into God's law for free men, he will not only remember it but he will do what it says, and God will greatly bless him in everything he does.

James 1:22–25 TLB

61

It says here, we don't need to be afraid to look into God's mirror because it actually "sets us free" when we look properly.

God's Mirror One of the first things we need to understand about God's perspective is that it is different from ours. He says, ". . . I do not judge as man judges. Man looks on the outward appearance, but I look at the heart" (1 Samuel 16:7). This does not mean that our bodies are unimportant to God. In fact, the opposite is true: ". . . The body is . . . for the Lord, and the Lord for the body" (1 Corinthians 6:13 NIV). God custom made our bodies. He determined how tall we would be, the size brain we would have, and our basic level of intelligence. He prescribed our facial features and handpicked the home into which we would be born. All these things outside of our control are very much inside of God's control. They are important to God, but they are not the most important things to Him. He is most concerned with our hearts—with what is inside.

- When you receive a present, what is more important to you: the wrapping paper or the gift inside?
- When you get a letter from someone special, what is more important: the envelope, or the message inside?
- When you are hungry, what is more important: the peel or the banana? The husk or the ear of corn? The shell or the peanut? The bun or the burger? Or when you are thirsty, what is more important, the bottle or the soda inside?
- When you look at a work of art, what is more important, the frame or the picture inside?

- When you think of *home*, what is more important, the cement blocks and shingles, or what's inside?

Obviousy, it's what's *inside* that counts. As important as the wrapper is, the contents are greater.

Everything in our society places the emphasis on the external—the superficial—so that it takes a conscious effort to see underneath the surface the way God does. As Christians, it is beautiful that we can see the interrelationship between the physical (the external) and the spiritual (the internal). While there is a difference, there is no dichotomy. When God made us, He put the right wrapper around the right contents; He put the right frame around the right picture; He put the right body around the right spirit. Wouldn't it be gross to open a banana peel and find an ear of corn inside? Or imagine opening a soda bottle and finding it full of peanut butter . . . you'd never get it out. Just as manufacturers choose the right packaging for the right product, so artists carefully choose the right frame for the right picture. The frame must not draw attention to itself, but rather to the painting. In the same way, God has lovingly and carefully given to us just the right body and human abilities through which we can best show forth the inner picture.

Now that we have a bit of God's perspective, let's see exactly who we are.

We Are Unique The first thing we need to understand about ourselves is that we are unique. You can look and look and look and never find another one like it. You are *it*.

In a sense, we could all wear buttons that say, "Special," "Custom-Made," "Handcrafted," "One of a Kind," "An

Original," "Made by the Master Craftsman." When God made us, He didn't look through back issues of *Sports Illustrated* or *Seventeen* to come up with ideas. When he creates a woman, He does not take the eyebrows of Brooke Shields, the body of Cheryl Tiegs, the brains of Sandra Day O'Connor, and the pedigree of Lady Di. He starts from scratch. When He makes a man, He doesn't take the speed of Carl Lewis, the agility of Doctor J, the stamina of Pete Rose, and tongue of Howard Cosell. After He made them, He threw away their blueprints. And before He made us, He drew up another whole set. We are unique.

The Bible says, "You created every part of me; you put me together in my mother's womb. . . . When my bones were being formed, carefully put together in my mother's womb, when I was growing there in secret, you knew that I was there—you saw me before I was born. The days allotted to me had all been recorded in your book, before any of them ever began" (Psalms 139:13, 15, 16). This expresses a sophisticated scientific truth. Scientists tell us that through the chromosomes and genetic structure within the mother's womb, essentially everything about us—body, mind, coordination, looks—is all there. And who is responsible for it? That's right, the Master Craftsman. He has never made two people exactly alike, and He never will.

We Are Special Almost every object bears the manufacturer's name. Automobiles, TVs, stereos, radios, cassette players all bear the names of their makers. Sneakers, T-shirts, jeans are all name branded. Books show the author, comics show the artist, and movies show the director. We as humans also bear the mark of our Maker.

The reason the products bear the manufacturer's mark is

because the maker is proud of his product. We need to understand that God is pleased with us, too.

One of the greatest enemies of this truth of creation is the myth of evolution. Teaching the survival of the fittest, evolution says that we are nothing more than a high level of animal, and too many teenagers run around high schools feeling like monkeys.

The best description of the myth of evolution that I have ever heard was at a Larry Norman concert. He said, "Expecting me to believe in evolution—that we all evolved from fungus—is like expecting me to believe that there was a paper factory on one side of the street and an alphabet soup company on the other side of the street; at exactly the same moment both companies blew up, with the soup noodles flying in the air on one side and the rolls of paper flying in the air on the other, landing on each other in the middle and printing the *Encyclopedia Britannica.*" When I heard that I roared.

No, my friend, you are not a monkey, and you are definitely not an overgrown fungus. You are human. You are special. You are not a chance; you are a creation. You were created in God's image, and you bear the mark of your Maker.

This might be hard to swallow, but when God made us, He made us in His image to resemble Him—to look like Him. Here is how the account goes: "Then God said, 'And now we will make human beings; they will be like us and resemble us.' ... So God created human beings, making them to be like himself...." And again it describes the distinctive creation of man this way, "Then the Lord God took some soil from the ground and formed a man out of it; he breathed life-giving breath into his nostrils and the man began to live" (Genesis 1:26, 27; 2:7).

Regardless of how literally you take this account, there is no way anyone can miss the fact that we as humans are categorically distinct from fungus and gorillas and the rest of God's creation. In a special way we were designed to know God personally and to have intimate fellowship with Him.

No one who has ever lived is a disaster. No one is a zero, a nerd, a worthless piece of trash. As the saying goes, "I'm somebody, 'cause God don't make no junk." It was true of Adam and Eve, and it's true of me and you. God treats us special because He made us and that should help us appreciate ourselves.

An Honest Look There are certain books that do a psych job. Some authors jump up and down and scream in your ear, trying to convince you that you are as smart as Einstein or as appealing and cute as Donny and Marie Osmond. When I read stuff like that I say, "Believe that, and I'll sell you some ocean-front property in Iowa."

When God shows us who we are, He doesn't lie. He doesn't fake us out or hide the truth from us. He doesn't give us only a partial picture or expect us to look through rose-colored glasses. He wants us to see ourselves exactly the way we are—warts and all! Listen to this: ". . . Do not think of yourself more highly than you ought, but rather think of yourself with sober judgment . . ." (Romans 12:3 NIV). God wants to impress us with who we are, but He doesn't want us to get overimpressed. He says, "Think of yourself with sober judgment," and that means be realistic, be honest. God is not fantasy. He is reality, and He expects us to see ourselves for who we are, even when that is less than impressive.

We all have our insecurities. When it comes to being a

physical specimen, no one scores a perfect "10." If we look close enough, we all have some defect—a mole, a few warts, some untimely pimples, freckles, wrinkles, scars, or scabs. But just because we might have a scab does not mean we are a scab. In fact, our defects and weaknesses are designed to help us each maintain our uniqueness.

An important part of finding out who I am, is discovering who I am not. Learning that I am not the greatest ball player since Babe Ruth, the prettiest face since Marilyn Monroe, the funniest comedian since Rodney Dangerfield, or the best songwriter since Bob Dylan is all part of discovering who I am. At first such a discovery might knock us off our high horse, but that is only because God wants to get our feet on the ground.

A Closer Look   When some kids hear about uniqueness, they say, "Unique? Yeah, right! I wish I wasn't so unique." What do you tell a kid who gets a true picture of what he's like, but instead of drooling on the mirror, he feels more like vomiting?

This reminds me of the lady who went to have her portrait taken at a fine studio. She spent the morning at the beauty parlor and the early afternoon at the cosmetologist. The photographer took her picture from every possible angle. When the proofs came back, the lady took one look and she was crushed. She didn't like any of them. "Sir," the lady sobbed, "none of these pictures does me justice." The photographer responded, "Lady, you don't need justice; you need mercy!"

We can snicker at this story but what do we do when we have an accurate view of ourselves and we just can't stand what we see? After all, the camera does not lie. Let's face it, there are certain things about ourselves that make us feel lousy: our parents' divorce, something about our physical appearance (crooked teeth, oversized nose, scrawny body), or our lack of personality or natural ability. These are exactly what God's Book is all about. His Book is written to help us handle the warts, the flops, and the insecurities. God's Book is the only place we can look to get an accurate picture of who we are, and at the same time, get an appreciation to accept it. God gives us both justice and mercy.

Let's Face It The best way to know if you have really accepted yourself is to start by facing your ugliest, weakest, and most insecure point: For some it might be your looks; for others it might be your abilities; for others it might be your parents.

The best way to discover which area this might be for you is to ask the question, *If I had the power to change anything about myself, what would it be?* Right now, think about it. Take a second, close your eyes, and answer the question. Imagine writing that word in this space: _____.

Facing that area head-on is justice, and it's hard. We know that if we were in control, it would have been different. Since God is in control, we are really holding a secret grudge against Him for doing such a lousy job. A girl at camp once told me, "If God is so powerful and so loving, why am I such a mess? If what I see in the mirror is an example of God's creativity, forget it!" She saw herself, but only partially. She got justice but not mercy.

When we see ourselves as God sees us, looking below the surface into our spirit and character, we begin to understand that all the defects and scars on the surface are intended to develop inner beauty. Since God is greatly concerned about both our body and our spirit, He never allows any blemish to the body that will damage the spirit. He is kind and sensitive to allow only certain physical traits to exist in us that are intended to produce godly character—to resemble Him!

God does this with such skill and sensitivity that the exact area that we had resented and would have changed if possible is the area for which God wants us actually to be grateful. Rather than regarding it as an enemy, you can welcome it as a friend. Rather than seeing it as a scar, it becomes a beauty mark, or a mark of God's ownership.

Let's Do It Before you set this book on your nightstand, you have something you need to do. Remember what God says, "... For if a person just listens and doesn't obey, he is like a man looking at his face in a mirror; as soon as he walks away, he can't see himself anymore or remember what he looks like" (James 1:23, 24 TLB).

Now that you have seen yourself in God's mirror, don't just fall asleep and forget, but act on it. Use this prayer to tell God how you feel

Father, I thank You for making me such a special person. You did a good job. I especially thank You for ... [name the area of your life you would have changed]. I admit I have resented this and have blamed You for it, but now I see it differently. It is a mark of Your ownership, and You want to make me look more like You. Since You designed me, I want You to be seen in me by others. I know that the inner person of my heart is the most important, so I want You to build Christlike character in me. Again, God, thank You for doing such a wonderful job putting me together.

In Jesus' Name, I love You.

 **Thoughts**

1. How is God's perspective different from ours?
2. Is our body important to God? Why?
3. "When God made us, He put the right wrapper around the right contents; He put the right frame around the right picture; He put the right body around the right spirit." Comment.
4. How can the myth of evolution give us a distorted view of ourselves?
5. Do you know anyone who has an unrealistically high view of himself? Describe the person. How does he make you feel?
6. Define *pride*. What does pride have to do with seeing ourselves accurately?
7. When it comes to facing who we really are, what is "justice"? "Mercy"?
8. How can a "scar" become a "beauty mark"?

 **Feelings**

1. Be honest. What defect do you have (physically, socially, athletically, academically)? How does it make you feel about yourself?
2. If you had the power to change anything about yourself, what would it be?
3. Most likely, this area is beyond your control, which means it is in God's control. To resent this part of your life is to resist God's creative handiwork. Believing that God is very concerned about both our bodies and our spirits and that He never allows any blemish to the body that will damage the spirit, could you, right now, thank Jesus for this area of your life? (Go back and reread the suggested prayer that finishes the chapter.)

70

6 My Hero

THEY'LL NEED A MUCH BIGGER ROCK TO DO JESUS!

MT. RUSHMORE

GREAT AMERICAN HEROES

OUR GENERATION LACKS a hero: someone to admire, look up to, and even imitate. When I was a kid, Roger Maris became a popular hero when he hit sixty home runs in one season. But then he lost the touch, got booed out of Yankee Stadium, and reportedly lost his hair due to a nervous condition. The Beatles, the great prophets and pop singers became idols. But they frequently changed religions, and soon after singing "All You Need Is Love," they split up. Then it was Farrah Fawcett, but she was unable to keep a boyfriend and ended up pregnant with Ryan O'Neal's baby. After being let down by all this world's glamour stars, where can you find a pure-bred hero?

Who is your hero? Mr. T.? Michael Jackson? Wonder Woman? When it comes to choosing a hero, we need to be careful where we look. We need to be sure he won't fall off his pedestal. The world has already seen too many Humpty-Dumpty heroes.

We have already seen that no other person is really big enough to ultimately make us feel good about ourselves, including coaches, teachers, parents, and friends. They are here today, but they may be gone tomorrow. The same is certainly true of our superheroes. But, in a world where heroes fail us and friends forsake us, Jesus comes along and says, ". . . I will never fail you nor forsake you" (Hebrews 13:5 RSV). And He means it.

Sometimes thinking about God can make insecure people feel even more insecure. They argue, "What does God know about failure? He's never lost at anything. He's the *Almighty;* what does he know about weakness, insecurity, and inferiority? He can't identify with the way I feel, and I can't identify with Him." In case you have ever had thoughts like this, let me refresh your memory.

Jesus, the Failure By many standards Jesus was a flop. He would hardly have been voted "most likely to succeed" by His graduating class. Just consider His résumé.

Physically, Jesus was no runt, but He probably would not have been on the cover of any fashion magazines. While no one ever took His picture, or painted His portrait, here is one less-than-flattering description of Him. He grew up ". . . like a plant taking root in dry ground. He had no dignity or beauty to make us take notice of him. There was nothing attractive about him, nothing that would draw us to him. We despised him and rejected him; he endured suffering and pain. No one would even look at him—we ignored him as if he were nothing" (Isaiah 53:2, 3).

Rather than pursuing His stepfather's business career as a carpenter, He became a traveling evangelist. He never owned a home, never rose to a position of influence or accumulated any money. The people in His hometown thought He was strange. They were convinced He had lost his marbles and saw Him as a stargazer, fortune-teller, and gypsy. He was such an embarrassment, they grabbed Him, led Him to the top of a hill, and tried to throw Him to His death.

The religious establishment saw Him as a terrorist—a fanatic, a radical who was leading a subversive plot to undermine their traditions. Soon after they first laid their eyes on Jesus, they knew they had to exterminate Him. He was a menace to society like a wild dog with rabies.

The king, having only heard rumors, requested a visit with Jesus, expecting Him to perform like a court jester or acrobat. When Jesus failed to pull rabbits from hats or saw people in half, the king felt insulted.

When they heard His name, the local politicians' skin crawled because Jesus spelled trouble for them. The Jewish leadership hated Jesus, and yet the Jewish common folk seemed to love the guy. At the end when it came down to a decison, the mayor flipped a coin and then washed his hands when it turned up tails.

He was called disgusting names like "Blasphemer," "God of Manure," "Drunkard," "Friend of Freaks," and "Criminal." People in positions of influence told vicious lies about Him, falsely accusing Him of fraud and treason. After being found innocent before those capable of sentencing Him to death, He was hung up like a side of beef in front of a howling mob that screamed, "Kill Him! Away with Him! He's a mangy dog! Kill Him!"

At the end things even got worse. Thirty-three years old—right in the prime of His life—He did not exactly die of natural causes. They ripped the skin off His back with a whip that looked something like barbed wire and spit their mucus on His open wounds. They made Him carry His own wooden beam to a garbage dump on the outskirts of town. Metal stakes crushed through His wrists and ankles, but suspended in midair, the nails could hardly hold the weight of His body. They stripped Him naked, gambled for His clothes, tore whiskers from His chin, splashed vinegar in His face, hurled ugly names, thrust a spear between His ribs, and mockingly hummed a few bars of "Amazing Grace."

When His popularity bottomed out, even His closest friends ran for the hills and hid themselves in shame. Jesus became a bad name, and they didn't want anything to do with him.

As He hung on the tree, dripping blood, His lungs filled up with fluid, and His head pounded with fever. He was barely able to get His breath. People gathered like vultures around His body, still belching out words like, "What a waste!" "What a weirdo!" "What a flop!"

Soon He died.

This description of Jesus' life might shatter your stained-glass view, but it is accurate. Such a list of accomplishments is not your average success story. At least they permanently lay to rest the idea that Jesus knew nothing about weakness and failure. Since He has identified with us in our insecurities, it should be much easier for all of us to identify with Him.

Jesus, the Success Even though, according to most standards, Jesus was a failure, there was Someone who was impressed—His Father. In fact, He was most impressed. We can accurately say of Jesus, He was a smashing success. He accomplished everything He wanted to do, even though He faced enormous obstacles.

Jesus never tried to impress people. All He ultimately wanted was to please His Father. At least two times during His life, He heard His Father say, "You are my beloved Son, with You I am well pleased." At the end of His life Jesus could say to His Dad, "I have accomplished the work You gave Me to do."

The final proof that His Father was impressed did not come until after He was dead, partially embalmed, and lying in the grave. God brought Him back to life. Essentially, God was saying, "Hey, everybody, My Son is no flop. He is the ultimate hero. Though you made His name a curse word, I have made it the most important name in the universe. Someday every one of you will get on your knees and admit that Jesus is the greatest" (*see* Philippians 2:5–11).

In Jesus we see a great reversal. What man often considers successful, God considers failure. And what God considers success, man often regards as a total waste. The very reason people rejected Jesus and considered Him a weirdo, was the exact same reason His Father was saying, "Well done." It is all a matter of values.

We pick our heroes based on our own values. If we see physical strength and coordination as the most important qualities in life, we will pick an athlete or muscle builder to be our hero. If we value physical beauty and sex appeal to be most important, we will pick a Hollywood star or beauty queen as our hero. If pure popularity means the most to us, we will simply choose whomever everyone else picks to be our hero, too. Since, however, we have already determined that all these areas are not of first importance, we need to find someone who has the right inner qualities to be our hero. His name is Jesus. Since He is the Source, why not look up to Him? You don't have to worry, He will not fall off His pedestal.

We, the Reason I can hear you asking a good question: "If Jesus was such a success, why didn't the people recognize it? Why was He such a failure?" This might surprise you, but *we* are the reason.

In a sense, Jesus became a nobody so that we nobodies might become somebodies. Jesus became a reject so that we rejects might be found. Jesus became a failure so that we failures might become successful. Jesus became a loser so that we losers might become winners.

Think about what it says in the Book:

- Though He was rich, yet for our sake, He became poor so that He might make us rich.

  See 2 Corinthians 8:9
- He became of no reputation so that we of no reputation might become known to God.

  See Philippians 2:7
- Cursed is everyone who hangs on a tree. Jesus became cursed so that we, the cursed, might be blessed.

  See Galatians 3:13, 14
- God made him to be sin who knew no sin so that we sinners might become the righteousness of God.

  See 2 Corinthians 5:21

Only Jesus can take a *has-been* and make Him a *will-be*. Jesus can make everything new; even you.

When we get down on ourselves, feeling depressed, forsaken, rejected, lonely, blue, we always have a place to go and Someone to talk to who understands just how we feel. His name is Jesus.

Jesus specializes in flops. He didn't come to save the success stories, but the nobodies, the nerds, the weirdos. The whole message of the Bible is that God puts us back together again. There is no one in God's book of success stories whose life was not reassembled.

The world puts us in one of two boxes, marked "winner" or "loser." The one box is put on the pedestal and the other box is put in the garbage disposal. Vince Lombardi, the legendary coach of the Green Bay Packers stated, "There's no room for second place. There is only one place, and that's first place." And again, "Winning isn't everything; it is the only thing."

The world has no place for losers, but aren't you glad Jesus does? He can change anybody. ". . . If any man is in Christ, he becomes a new creature; old things pass away, behold all things become new" (*see* 2 Corinthians 5:17).

When I Grow Up . . . For some of us, it is time to change heroes; to take down the posters of rock stars and athletes and put Jesus in their place. He has all the stuff out of which real heroes are made.

- He stood alone against enormous odds.
- He looked death square in the face and would not flinch when the devils roared.
- When every cell cried "Quit," He refused to listen.
- He refused to compromise His conviction even when it meant losing friends and suffering physical injury.

Jesus has all the strength and guts out of which heroes are made, and unlike other people, His abilities and popularity do not decrease with age. His dignity and beauty don't get old.

When someone asks you the question, "Who do you want to be like when you grow up?" feel free to say, *"Jesus."*

A Lesson From Mickey Mantel Every kid dreams of getting close to his hero. When we go to a game, we hope to get an autograph. When we go to concerts, we hope for a handshake or maybe a picture. It is exciting to have personal contact with our idol; it makes us feel special.

As a kid, I loved baseball so I always kept my eye on Mickey Mantel. I could hardly believe it when I received a postcard signed by him. Every week I got a card from him. Then I noticed the postmark was from my hometown. "Mom, does Mickey Mantel live near us?" It didn't take long until I realized Mickey Mantel was really Santa Claus—my father! I was crushed.

Jesus is different. He is a hero we can get close to, but He will never let us down. He said He wants to be our friend. He doesn't just send us postcards or shake our hands in passing. He doesn't make us stand in line to get His autograph. In fact, He comes to us in person. He says, "Here I am! I stand at the door and knock. If anyone hears my voice and opens the door, I will come in and eat with him, and he with me" (Revelation 3:20 NIV).

The one who helps us accept ourselves wants us to accept Him. He created us physically, and He wants to recreate us spiritually. The more comfortable we feel with Him, the more courage and confidence we have to turn ourselves over to His control.

We can all look up to Jesus like a big brother and say, "When I grow up, I want to be just like You."

Thoughts

1. On what basis do most of your friends choose heroes? What qualities do their heroes exhibit? What values are represented?
2. How does the sin of "idolatry" apply to teen idols? How can today's superheroes put our focus on the wrong things?
3. What qualities qualify Jesus to be a true hero?
4. In what ways was Jesus a failure? A success?
5. "Jesus became a nobody so that we nobodies might become somebodies." Explain.
6. How is Jesus superior to any other hero?

Feelings

1. After reading the section "Jesus, the Failure," how did it make you feel toward Him? What was the most surprising part of that section?
2. "Since Jesus has identified with us in our insecurities, it should be much easier for all of us to identify with Him." Respond. Does it make it easier for you to identify with Him?
3. List a few of your heroes. Are they morally upright? Do they exhibit the right inner qualities required to be considered true heroes?
4. What do you admire most about Jesus?
5. How do you respond to Jesus when He says, "Listen, I stand at the door and knock; if anyone hears my voice and opens the door, I will come into his house"? Have you heard His voice? Opened the door to your life? Have you enjoyed Him living inside of you?

7 Failing God

WE NEVER WANT to succeed as much as when our hero is watching. When our girl friend is in the bleachers, we try harder. When our parents are proudly standing in the crowd, we want to do our best.

Imagine Sugar Ray Leonard cheering for you at ringside and you get knocked out in the first round. Or imagine Don Shula standing on the sidelines, watching you throw three interceptions. You'd feel like a jerk. You had such great opportunity to shine like a superstar but you fizzed out.

In the same way, when we really want to please Jesus but then wipe out, it hurts. Knowing He was watching the whole thing makes it even worse.

Peter loved Jesus, and he loved to have a good time. He was a natural leader and most of his friends didn't mind following. He usually attended the youth meetings and played a mean trombone at church. To put it mildly, his mother was very upset when for the first time, he came home drunk. The second time he came in drunk, he was lucky she didn't skin him alive. Not knowing what else to do, she asked me to talk with him which I did.

"Hey, I know what God wants me to do, so don't start in on that jazz," he warned me, trying to establish some ground rules. I agreed, so he continued: "It's not that I like what I'm doing. I don't. It makes me feel so guilty I could puke . . . and I don't even like the taste of beer."

I just let him continue talking; he was doing fine. "You know what? I even love Jesus. I know He is the only way to get to heaven, and I know He is the only way to be happy. I can't handle it anymore. I'm just tired of being such a disappointment to Him. I feel like I'm letting everyone down. I let the other kids at church down. I let my parents down. And worst of all, I know I let God down. I'm just a big let-down!" He cried, "I just couldn't stand disappointing God again."

"Peter, God will forgive you," I said.

"Yeah, I know He will. That's what makes it even worse. Don't you understand, it is harder knowing that He still loves me. If He hauled off and clobbered me once, I think it would make me feel better."

It became very clear that his guilt over past failure had become a wedge between him and God, and God's love was almost like a hammer driving it deeper and deeper.

Spiritual Wipeouts Anyone who has ever desired to please God has at some point displeased Him. At Christian camp we make a very sincere commitment: "No Bible, no breakfast." We want to get up and spend time reading the Bible before school and we do pretty good for a couple of weeks. But the alarm doesn't go off one morning or at least we don't hear it, so we failed once. Then the next morning we condemn ourselves, "Jerk! You broke the promise once, so what's the use?" We sleep in again. Soon we are hardened losers, fully convinced we'll never go anywhere with God.

We listen to a ripsnorting message, making us feel guilty

for not telling others about Jesus. "God, I promise to tell my best friend about You tomorrow." What happens? We choke before class. We put it off during lunch, and by the time school is out, we have forgotten all about the promise. The next time some preacher tries to tell us about witnessing we say under our breath, "Forget it! I've already tried."

At church we get convicted about worldliness and vow to give up smoking, drinking, drugs, dancing, rock 'n roll, and even AM radio. That might sound good on Sunday, but from Monday to Saturday it's not that easy. You get in your friend's car after school which appears innocent enough. She flips on the radio, and Michael Jackson jumps out singing "Beat It." "What do I do . . . man, it's her car . . . it's her radio . . . there's no way she'd understand if I told her." Your conscience says its wrong but you can't beat it. There's nowhere to go. You feel trapped, so you slightly lower your standard. The next time she gives you a ride, she asks you to reach into the glove compartment, get the plastic bag, and roll her a joint. What will you say? You will probably roll the reefer and rationalize, "Why not? As long as I don't smoke it, what will it hurt?" And then there will be the next time.

Most of us can identify with these feelings—feeling like a spiritual zero, an infidel. Peter certainly could. That day as he and I talked, he went through each of the steps outlined in this chapter, and he went from failure to spiritual victory. Let's follow it, inch by inch.

Step 1: To Confess Beats Success (The Myth of the Super-Christian) Peter burst out, "Fred, you are too much! You really think God can do something with me, huh?" I guess my king-size smile bothered him. "Well, I've got news for you, I am a real loser . . . a total flop when it comes to the Jesus stuff. I stink at prayer. I totally freeze when somebody calls on me to pray in Sunday school. That's why I quit going. I can't understand a thing in the Bible . . . it puts me to sleep. I swear. I wish I didn't, but I have a temper, and when I get mad, the words just come out. I think bad thoughts about other people . . . especially girls. When I go to church, it makes me feel like a hypocrite. And witnessing . . . aw, man! I am a total klutz. I try to tell my friends about Jesus, but I fumble for words. You know me, I can talk about anything so why can't I talk about Jesus? It's not like I don't know the Guy."

As I listened, I had to resist chuckling out loud. I coudn't believe my ears. Peter reminded me so much of Jesus' disciple with the same name. I was hearing a wonderful expression of honesty and confession.

"Peter, you have just taken the first giant step in the right direction." He looked back at me as if I just told him a lie. But I kept talking, "Your biggest problem is not your spiritual failure but rather your failure to bring your spiritual failure to God. Hey, I know it's hard to tell Him about our flops especially when it's not the first time." By the half-grin and the rolling eyeballs, I could tell he identified.

Stephen Olford is one of the great preachers of our generation. I was listening to one of his tapes the other day, and I couldn't believe my ears. He said, "The most important truth I have learned about the Christian life is this: The only thing that God ever expects from Stephen Olford is utter failure." I thought I must have gotten it wrong, so I ran over to the cassette player, punched "rewind," and listened again; then, a third time. Initially, I wasn't sure I even agreed with the statement, but when he said it was the *most important* thing he has learned about the Christian life, that really threw me.

He proceeded to quote the Bible, "For I know that nothing good dwells within me, that is, in my flesh. I can will what is right, but I cannot do it" (Romans 7:18 RSV). "The sooner we understand that the Christian life is impossible, the sooner we can turn our insufficiencies over to God's all-sufficiency." The light went on, and I saw it. God can turn our failure into victory. His strength mixed with our weakness becomes our strength.

I told Peter, "You show me a *super-Christian*, and I'll show you a faker. In fact, guys who strut around acting like they are hot stuff, parading their Sunday-school perfect-attendance pins as if they were spiritual merit badges, turn God off. Don't ever think you need to impress God in order to win His approval. The only thing you need to do in order to get God's attention is to be honest . . . and you are honest with yourself. Now, you just need to be convinced that God loves you anyway."

I read him these words of Jesus, "People who are well do not need a doctor, but only those who are sick. I have not come to call respectable people, but outcasts" (Mark 2:17).

I knew he was catching on because he said, "That sure includes me."

Step 2: *Progress Beats Success* (*The Myth of the Professional Christian*) Here is another hard lesson for us to learn: Our *success* does not mean as much to God as our *progress*.

The president of my seminary was Dr. Harold J. Ockenga, a very distinguished gentleman everyone looked at as being a great man of God. He was so dignified that it was hard to believe he ever had any problems. One day he shared with some of the students, "We all need patience as we grow in Christ. As a young man, I was a great competitor in sports and I had a bad temper. Those two were a bad combination, and for many years I struggled with swearing. Even for years after I met Jesus as my Saviour, I would miss a jump shot in the gym and a word would slip out." (I had held him in such high esteem, at first I was almost disappointed. But then it hit me, "He's human!")

Even though God wants us holy, He never wants us to forget that we are human. We will all disappoint Him. We will all fall on our faces. We will all make mistakes. He knows all about it anyway, so we might as well be honest and patient, knowing that no kid grows up overnight.

Since Peter was a good musician I asked him, "When you first started playing the trombone, did you ever hit any bad notes?" He agreed. "Okay, so why didn't you quit? What about a recital—your first recital—did you make any mistakes?" He agreed he made a bunch. "Wasn't that embarrassing?" He agreed. "How about now? Are you in a band?" He played first trombone in the all-state orchestra. "So your patience paid off, huh?" He agreed. "And I bet your parents got sick of hearing you play flat and sharp notes for the first few years, huh? And your sister and brother, too? In fact, I bet the church had to put up with a few mistakes when you played there the first time?" By now he knew I was on to something. He was looking at me suspiciously because he knew it was coming.

I didn't disappoint him: "So what makes you think you are going to be a professional Christian right away? Don't you think you'll ever hit a few wrong notes? It seems to me that it is natural for your parents and friends and church members to hear you goof up once in a while ... in fact, they might hear you goof up quite frequently, but that doesn't mean you get kicked out of the band." He seemed to eat it up.

"God is not as impressed with professional Christians as He is with progressing Christians. He doesn't want us to feel as if we are always in the spotlight, performing; He just wants us to live with Him and practice and pretty soon it starts coming naturally. The same patience you have with your music, you need to have with your Lord. And don't feel like you're a hypocrite when you hit a wrong note; it just means you're human."

Step 3: To Submit Brings Success (Three Strikes Is Not an Out) Peter, the rugged fisherman who left his nets to follow Jesus, is a classic example of a spiritual klutz. He had a violent temper and became famous for his coordination at putting his foot in his mouth. He had giant mood swings up and down; he dared to walk on water, but then sank; he was the first to say that Jesus was the Christ but then blew it by saying He must never die; at first he refused to allow Jesus to wash his feet and then requested that He give him a bath; and at the end he vowed on a stack of Bibles he'd never deny Christ and within twenty-four hours made the *Guinness Book of World Records* by denying Him three times. Well, praise the Lord, in God's league, three strikes does not mean you are out. In fact, in Peter's case, he became the clean-up hitter. Jesus said only of Peter, "You are the rock on which I will build my church." Frankly, some who heard that must have thought Jesus had rocks in His head for making such a choice. "How could He choose such an inconsistent, emotional roller coaster like Peter?" they thought.

When Jesus looked right into his eyeballs after he had denied Him the third time, Peter was brought face to face with his own humanity, and it hurt. In fact, it hurt so badly that he went off and cried his eyes out. Peter certainly was human, but he was no hypocrite—he was no faker.

The apostle was painfully aware that he was a flop, but his whole life changed when he realized that Jesus wasn't through with him. We don't know all the details, but a few days after Jesus died and Peter had gone back to fishing, rumors began to circulate that He had come back to life.

The day was hot, they were not even getting a nibble, and Peter had stripped down to his gym shorts. Some out-of-towner calls from the beach, "Any luck?" When the negative answer came back, he suggested, "Try the starboard side!" They probably said to themselves, "There is a smart aleck in every crowd," but they had nothing to lose, so they gave it a try. The film crew from "That's Incredible" should have been there. The lines got tight, the water got dark with the slimy bodies of fish, and the boat began to tip. Unbelievable! Peter looked back to the beach with a grin as wide as his boat, and screamed, "Wow, it's *Jesus!*" He grabbed his T-shirt and swam to shore. That day he learned two things that changed his life forever: (1) Jesus was risen from the dead; and (2) He does not give up on anybody.

After telling Peter this story about the disciple with the same name, I asked him, "Right now, do you know that Jesus loves you? That He hasn't give up on you?" He only nodded but by the light in his eyes, I knew he meant it. "Do you believe that Jesus is risen from the dead and that He is able to do for you what you could never do for yourself?"

"Yup."

That day marked a turning point in Peter's life. He was not a finished product. In fact, the only thing that really changed was the way he saw himself. Rather than being a hypocrite, he was a human and he was honest about it. Rather than being a flop because he was not an instant success, he saw himself in a process of progress. Before he left, with tears running down his cheeks, he prayed a prayer I will never forget . . . "God, You are too much. I don't understand why You love me, but I know You do. I can't figure out why You haven't given up on me long ago, or why You ever wanted me in the first place. Even when I rejected You, You never rejected me. But as long as You don't mind having me, I give myself to You. I guess I'm not the biggest project You've got, but I sure feel like it. I'm sorry for all the times I've blown it. I hate the way I've hurt my parents and the way I have let down my Christian friends. It's not going to be easy starting all over again, and it probably won't be the last time either . . . only next time I think I'll remember this stuff so that I won't wait so long. I guess I've been harder on myself than You have. Now, since I'm so weak, You're going to have to help. I don't mind a few mistakes along the way, but I sure want to get better. I don't mind being embarrassed once in a while, as long as I see a little improvement. Thanks for being so patient. I really do love You, Jesus. Amen."

Thoughts

1. Do you know anyone like Peter? Describe him or her.
2. Why does it hurt so badly when we disappoint God?
3. Describe a "super-Christian."
4. What does it mean to "confess"?
5. "Your biggest problem is not your spiritual failure but rather your failure to bring your spiritual failure to God." Discuss.
6. Describe a "professional Christian."
7. "Our success does not mean as much to God as our progress." Respond.
8. Give several examples in the apostle Peter's life that resemble Peter in this chapter.
9. How can spiritual failure get us down on ourselves?

Feelings

1. Did you ever feel like a fool by disappointing God? How?
2. Have you ever broken a promise or a commitment to God? What was it? How did you respond afterwards?
3. How does God want us to respond following our spiritual failures?
4. What makes returning to Jesus easier?

8 Ultimate Failure

WE WILL ALL take a final bow. The curtain will open, and there in front of us will be a giant mirror in which we will see ourselves for who we really are. For some of us it will be the first time.

A youth was jogging carefree down the sidewalk as he neared the elderly man. "How's it going old-timer?" the boy blurted.

The elder reached out, grabbed the kid by the shirt, and stopped him in his tracks, "Son, what are you going to do with your life?"

At first the kid was stunned. He quickly snapped out of it and responded, "Oh, I'm going to college next year."

The man did not let go, "Then what?"

"Oh, I'll go on to graduate school."

"Then what?"

The kid blushed and cleared his throat, "Oh, I guess I'll get a high-paying job, get married, buy a big house in the suburbs, and raise a family."

The kid was impressed by the answer, but the elder was not. "Then what?"

"Well, I'll lay up enough money for retirement and play with my grandchildren, I guess. . . ."

This time the man got up nose to nose, looked clear through the boy, and asked for the final time, "Then what?"

The youth could only stare at the old man's weathered face, and he started to sweat. Embarrassed that he had no ultimate answers to life, he took a big gulp, and walked away slowly.

I'm not an old man and I cannot grab your shirt, but I still want to ask you a deep question, "Then what?" I want you to look into the final mirror of eternity before it's too late. Until you know why you do the things you do, your life lacks meaning.

Temporal Success It is easy to think that the richest guys are the most successful, but some of those with millions of dollars have not had two bits of inner peace and fulfillment. Listen to what Bill Bright, founding president of Campus Crusade, recorded (*Revolution Now*, pp. 44, 45):

For example in 1923 a very important meeting was held at the Edgewater Beach Hotel in Chicago. Attending this meeting were nine of the world's most successful financiers: Charles Schwab, steel magnate; Samuel Insull, president of the largest utility company; Howard Hopson, president of the largest gas company; Arthur Cotton, the greatest wheat speculator; Richard Whitney, president of the New York stock exchange; Albert Fall, a member of the President's Cabinet; Leon Fraser, president of the Bank of International Settlements; Jesse Livermore, the great "bear" on Wall Street; and Ivar Krueger, head of the most powerful monopoly.

Twenty-five years later, Charles Schwab had died in bankruptcy, having lived on borrowed money for five years before his death; Samuel Insull had died a fugitive from justice and penniless in a foreign land;

Howard Hopson was insane; Arthur Cotton had died abroad, insolvent; Richard Whitney had spent time in Sing Sing; Albert Fall had been pardoned so that he could die at home: Jesse Livermore, Ivar Krueger and Leon Fraser had all died by suicide. All of these men had learned well the art of making a living, but none of them had learned HOW TO LIVE!

Listen to what Jesus said, "What does it profit a man if he gain the whole world and lose his own life" (*see* Mark 8:36). Being successful cannot be gauged by the size of your bank account, your circle of friends, or your sphere of influence. The dainties of this world were never intended to satisfy the hunger pains down deep in our hearts. You might impress a few people with your money, but someday you will look into the face of One who will say, "Big deal!" Temporal success alone is really failure.

Partial Success A partial success is someone who is a winner and yet at the same time feels like a loser.

We can get good at the popularity games and crowd pleasers that win fast friends. The problem is, we need to play the fool in order to win the game. Usually those who win such games are losers in life.

Our generation allows a guy to call premarital intercourse "a conquest." I knew a kid who made it his goal to "conquer" every girl he dated. That is not winning, that's losing. It is losing respect; it's losing dignity; it's losing purity. The only things "conquests" win are disease, guilt, boredom, loneliness, emptiness, depression, unwanted children, headaches, parent problems, and personal disrespect.

While I was growing up, as a Jets fan, my hero was Joe Namath. One day I even got to go into the locker room before the game and meet some of the players. Standing next to receiver Don Maynard made me feel like a shrimp and when I tried to shake Winston Hill's hand, I couldn't even make it around his third finger. I walked past the showers; there he stood in nothing more than a towel—Broadway Joe, himself.

He was a great passing quarterback with an almost instant release. In 1967 he set a record as being the only quarterback to pass for over 4,000 yards in a single season. In his book *I Can't Wait Until Tomorrow 'Cause I Get Better Looking Every Day,* he mentioned the game in which he set a season record by passing the most yards in a single game—close to 450. The reporters made a big deal about it, but there was only one problem—they lost the game.

What good does it do to set a record but lose the game? There were many passes caught that day, but not enough of them were caught in the end zone. Partial success is really failure. When we take our final curtain call, we will stand before the One who sees the whole picture and some of us will wish we'd spent more time living and less time playing foolish little games.

Flops in Hero Masks   What feeds a false view of success is phony heroes:

- Cold-blooded rock stars who gyrate on stage in front of thousands of drooling teenage lips, who leave unwed mothers and fatherless children at every pit stop
- The sex stars who appear as sweet as the innocent

girl next door, who are as sour as spinach juice on the inside
- The beer drinkers, the beauty queens, the pacesetters who are the first married and the first divorced, the first to kiss and the first to brag.

John Belushi, a star of "Saturday Night Live," was not the last of the red-hot lovers, but he did all right for himself. He had more than his share of women. One of his favorite sayings was, "Things go better with coke" (referring to the narcotic, not the soft drink). The night he overdosed on a fatal "speedball" (a heroin and cocaine cocktail), next to his corpse on the nightstand were a glass of wine and a script to a new movie in which he was due to star entitled, *The Joy of Sex.* It was too bad he died. Nevertheless another lie was not recorded on film—the lie that tells only half the story; the lie that shows the twenty-minute sexual sizzle but not the people who get burned in the process and certainly none of the scars. Even Belushi was quoted as saying, "I give so much pleasure to so many people. Why can't I get some pleasure for myself?"

We need to look seriously at our heroes and be willing to discover they have been wearing masks. It is disappointing to learn that certain superstars are moral washouts, but it is better to face the facts than to look up to a real loser.

Success Without Satisfaction   It does no good for others to tell us we are successful and to be honored with great rewards if we do not feel successful inside.

Many newspapers carried the closing remarks of a valedictorian of an Ivy League school that left the teeth of his entire graduating class rattling at their commencement exercises: "I have been at this university for four years," he said. "I have studied my courses; I have done all I could. But in these four years I have not found out what life is all about. I don't know why I am here. I don't know why I exist. And if anybody knows, I wish you would please come and tell me."

He was intelligent, considered outstanding among his peers, and was being honored with a diploma and special award. Yet the whole thing left a bad taste in his mouth. He had come to the end and had to honestly ask, "Is that all there is?" Inside he knew there must be more to life. Success without satisfaction is little reward. Hell is full of people who succeeded at the wrong things.

You want to know who are the real failures? They are the ones who spend their whole lives trying to win all the wrong races; the ones who get to the end of the rainbow only to find that the pot is full of maggots; the ones who clawed their way to the top of the ladder only to learn that it was leaning against the wrong building; maybe even worse, those who spent their lives drooling at such flops and calling them heroes. They are the ones who have really failed because they have failed themselves and they have failed God.

It's one thing for someone else to call you a flop, or even for you to call yourself a flop. But what happens when you come to the end of your life and God calls you a flop? That is ultimate failure, and that is hell. Then the party is over. The lights go out. We will have run the final lap of the last race, and for some of us, it will be the last gasp.

The ultimate failure is the one who chooses the wrong values to live by.

Thoughts

1. What are some different values by which to judge success?
2. What is a "moral failure"?
3. Which superstars are moral failures?
4. What is "partial success"?
5. Why is money not worth living for?
6. What is "ultimate failure"?
7. What do most of your friends look to for happiness?
8. "The ultimate failure is one who chose the wrong values to live by." Explain.
9. Which is more important, what friends think or what Jesus thinks? Why is it easy to choose pleasing our friends?

Feelings

1. If you tragically died in a car accident, how would you like to be remembered at your funeral?
2. What is big enough to spend your life living for?
3. What is the most important thing in your life?
4. What would it be like at the end of your life to hear Jesus say to you, "Depart from Me, I never knew you"?
5. Why does thinking seriously about eternity help us live more consistently?

9 Ultimate Success

WELL DONE, GOOD AND FAITHFUL SERVANT.

WOW!

A WASTE IS a teenager who quits too soon. One of the most pathetic sounds is a kid blowing his own whistle before the game is actually over. It's one thing for a kid to call time out—we all feel like taking a break once in a while. But when a kid decides it's time to throw in the towel because there is just no use in playing anymore, that is a waste. There is only one Person who is entitled to blow the final whistle, and He is the same One who blew the opening whistle.

Throughout this book I have been trying to convince you that you are too young to die. You are too young to come to the conclusion that you are a flop. You are too young to say, "I quit." Don't give up so easily on yourself; God hasn't.

Just think what would have happened if these people had quit too soon.

- Albert Einstein could not speak until he was four years old, and he couldn't read until he was seven. (What if he'd quit trying?)
- Beethoven's music teacher was quoted as saying, "As a composer, he is hopeless." (What if he'd listened?)
- Billy Sunday made major league baseball history when he struck out the fourteenth consecutive time (a record that still stands—no one is anxious to take it from him). Most people thought he was washed

107

up. He went on to become the highest paid ball player in his day, and the first player to circle the bases in twelve seconds. (What if he'd listened to the boos?)

- Thomas Edison did not do well in school. In fact, as a young boy his teacher said he would never learn anything. (Little did she know.)
- Enrico Caruso, Italian opera star, was told by one music teacher, "You can't sing. You have no voice at all." (Huh!)
- Walt Disney was fired by a newspaper editor because he was thought to have "no good ideas." (What a joke!)
- Jesse Burkett was a pitching disaster and was sent to the outfield to be a fly catcher. Five years later he made baseball history by finishing the season with a batting average of .423, and eventually batted himself into the Hall of Fame by hitting over .400 three different years (Some fly catcher!)
- Louisa May Alcott, author of several literary classics, was told by an editor that she would never write anything with popular appeal.
- F. W. Woolworth got a job in a store when he was twenty-one but was not allowed to wait on customers because he "did not have enough sense." (Maybe it was the store manager who didn't have any sense.)
- Willie Mays entered the major leagues on his twentieth birthday but didn't get a hit his first twelve times to the plate. He only got one hit his first twenty-six times at bat and held an unimpressive batting average of .038. Running for a fly ball, he

even knocked over a teammate. Willie said to his well-known boss, Leo Durocher, "You've made a big mistake bringing me up here.... You don't want me on your team. I am not good enough yet." However, by the end of the season, Willie lifted his batting average to .300 and swung the Giants into the pennant race. The rest of the story is history. (What if he had hung up his spikes too soon?)

• Abraham Lincoln's road to the White House was not exactly paved with success: bombed out at business in 1831; defeated for legislature in 1832; bombed at business again in 1833; had a nervous breakdown in 1836; defeated for speaker in 1838; lost as elector in 1840; lost at Congress in 1843; lost for Congress again in 1848; defeated for Senate in 1855; overturned for vice-president in 1856; lost at Senate again in 1858; elected president in 1860—considered the most successful president in our nation's history. (What if all his losses had convinced him that he was a loser?)

Our career at baseball isn't over just because we strike out or lose the game. Our education isn't through just because we flunk a course. Our future isn't washed up just because we get fired from our job. Just because we lose the election doesn't mean nobody cares.

One of the great philosophers of our day, Yogi Berra said, "The game isn't over until it's over." That is so simple it almost sounds stupid, but we all need to hear it. Everyone is bound to wipe out now and then, but we can all bounce back and be winners in the end.

A True Winner   Just as we have said that ultimate failure is choosing the wrong values, *ultimate success is choosing the right values by which to live.* Right values are not always popular values; in fact, to some people they will seem peculiar. Right values might even seem wrong to some people, but at least when we keep them consistently, they make us feel good about ourselves.

• *The Moral Success*   No one can be considered a human success if he is a moral failure. As we have seen, there is nothing victorious about sexual "conquests." In order to be truly successful, you need to be a moral success.

Susan became morally successful when she ended her relationship with Calvin because he wanted to have sex before marriage. Even though it meant losing the only boy in her life, she chose to be true to her convictions and lose Calvin rather than choosing Calvin and losing her self-respect.

Chris became morally successful soon after he dedicated his life to Jesus. He had made more than enough mistakes and had hurt more than enough girls, but Jesus forgave him and made him a new man. He not only changed his moral convictions and standards, but he telephoned those he had offended and received their forgiveness.

Leslie became morally successful when she was able to forgive herself and overcome her weakness by relying on Jesus' power inside. She hated herself for all her turbulent romances and especially for the abortion. She felt like a moral disaster. Rather than rambling, let me abbreviate her story: After receiving Christ, she read in the Bible that she was a new person. Even though she didn't feel like it, or act like it, she assumed it was true. As a new person,

Jesus gave her a new start, self-control, and a fresh sense of personal dignity. When she did date, every gland in her body begged, "Let him touch you, kiss you, caress you," but God's Book gave her strengthened conviction to say, "No."

Notice: we said that everyone "became" morally successful. No one is born that way. You can be born into a family worth millions of dollars and automatically become a financial success. However, to be a moral success requires a deliberate personal choice. You might have been born into a Christian home that taught you strict moral standards, but only *you* can decide to make them your own. Besides, unlike money, morality starts on the inside. Nobody can put a bat in your hands and expect you to be a professional baseball player, and no one can lay a set of moral principles on you and expect you to be pure. You have to want it. To be a moral success is a good goal for us to have.

Well-known baseball manager, Leo Durocher, said, "Show me a good loser, and I'll show you a loser." Fortunately with Jesus it is not so final. When we fail morally, we can admit it and receive Jesus' forgiveness. An important part of moral success is knowing that Jesus can make a winner out of a loser.

The moral success is the one who:

- is able to leave home without being afraid of his mother finding the dirty magazine he hid (because he isn't hiding any).
- does not have to sweat out his girl friend's pregnancy test (because his moral standard keeps him free from such fear—he is not physically involved).

- knows there are certain immodest clothing styles that are not right for her (even though her friends wear them).
- purposes in her heart to wait until marriage.
- is able to put his head on his pillow, turn out the light, and say, "Lord, it was great to be with You today."
- respects himself enough to keep himself pure, and treats others the same way.
- cares more about what Jesus in heaven thinks than what Joe Blow in homeroom thinks (even though Joe Blow has a big mouth).
- lets the absolute standard of God's Book determine what's right and wrong.

• ***The Permanent Success*** Many millionaires have flopped because money isn't everything. In order to be successful we need to be involved with something that outlasts us.

John Bechtel had so much potential that when he gave his life to be an aggressive missionary for Jesus Christ, people told him, "John, it's a waste. Anybody can be a missionary; you have too much talent for that. Stay here in America and make a mark for yourself."

After years of service in the overcrowded island of Hong Kong, he has seen many churches started, lives changed, a youth camp begun, the Bible school expanded, and many people put their faith in Jesus as Saviour. Still, businessmen there in Hong Kong have called him and said, "John, you have so much potential in a business career. We will give you a house overlooking Hong Kong Bay, a chauffeured limousine, and a salary of fifty thousand dollars if you work for us just as a consultant." When he said, "No," they came back at him, "How about seventy-five thousand?"

"No."

"Would you consider eighty-three thousand?"

Finally he explained, "Hey, you don't understand; the salary is fine, but the *job* is too small."

The question is this: "Is what you're living for worth Jesus' dying for?" John set his sights high and would not compromise himself, settling for temporal success when he could give his energies to lasting success—to helping people find meaning in life through Jesus Christ.

• *The Personal Success*   Those who are a personal success feel good about themselves for the right reasons. They have the inner satisfaction that they are fulfilling their God-given purpose in life to all their potential.

We can look at Amy Grant and ask, "Sure, why shouldn't she feel good about herself? She's pretty, talented, and rich." She has been a success by any standards, having won three Dove Awards and two Grammies. She is the only gospel musician to have received authorization for a gold album from the Recording Industry Association of American when "Age to Age" sold an incredible 500,000.

She says that the reason she feels good about herself is not because of her accomplishments, money, and looks. Her self-worth goes deeper than that. Listen: "Music is for me the enjoyable thing I do, and I feel God gave me the gift of enjoying singing. But it's like somebody saying I have pretty hair . . . I mean, I wash my hair, get out of the shower, run a brush through it—that's it. It has nothing to do with my merit as a person. The more I sing and the more people I sing to, honestly, the more insignificant I feel. As I grow in my relationship with the Lord and have a more realistic picture of who God is—we are talking peanuts, that's all we are" (*Christian Reader*, Nov./Dec. 1984, p. 5).

Even a success like Amy Grant does not base her merit as a person on what people think, but on what God thinks. Many stars have had great popularity but have felt like losers personally. It doesn't do any good to have the crowd on your side, if you don't have Christ. The personal success Amy Grant senses is because she has accepted herself and she knows Christ has also.

A hit song, "In a Little While," from her golden album, expresses where Amy's sights are set:

> Got a ticket coming home,
> wish the officer had known
> what a day today has been.
> Then I stumbled through the door,
> dropping junk-mail on the floor,
> when will this day end?
> But then your letter caught my eye,
> brought the hope in me to life,
> 'cause you know me very well,
> and I bet you wrote me,
> just to tell me
>
> In a little while we'll be with the Father,
> can't you see Him smile?
> In a little while we'll be home forever,
> in a while.
> We're just here to learn to love Him,
> we'll be home in just a little while.

© 1982 by Handrail Music/ASCAP, Addi Music/BMI, Meadowgreen Music Inc./ASCAP and Bug And Bear Music/ASCAP. All rights reserved. International copyright secured. Used by permission.

Amy Grant has set her sights on her ultimate reward.

Success Means Sacrifice Part of choosing where we will succeed is choosing where we are willing to fail. It is impossible to win all the games. You might as well decide now which ones you will play and which ones you will pass.

At every Olympics I am impressed by the amount of time and energy required from each of the athletes years in advance in order to compete. Each athlete is required to sacrifice many things: sleep, schooling, sweets, sweat, even friends in order to give themselves to their special event.

Some of Mary Lou Retton's friends probably thought she was taking her gymnastics much too seriously and missing out on all the fun. But at the Olympic awards ceremony when the gold medal was draped around her neck, honoring her as the best female gymnast in the world, everything she sacrificed along the way suddenly seemed worthwhile.

A sacrifice is "giving up something of value in order to get something of greater value." We can actually determine a person's value system by watching what he is willing to sacrifice.

When I decided to follow Jesus and wait to get my ultimate reward from Him, I also decided to forfeit some of the fanfare from the world. While I will win at life, I know I will not even play some of the games along the way, so according to certain standards, my life will be considered a waste. The exciting thing is that it doesn't matter who is booing along the way when I hear Jesus cheering for me at the finish line. If we lose sight of the final reward and start listening to our critics, our sacrifice will dwindle and our performance will suffer.

Even when we might trip up and suffer temporary defeat, we need to hear these words of preacher Peter Marshall: "It is better to fail at a cause that will ultimately succeed than to succeed at a cause that will ultimately fail."

A Lesson From Shakespeare When I was in college, I took two English courses in Shakespeare; the one was worse than the other. I enjoyed his humor and wit and the violence kept me from falling asleep but one thing I could never figure out was why some plays were called *comedy* and others *tragedy*. The entire play might be filled with one blood-and-guts scene after another, with hate and murder, tears and sorrow, and yet it would be called a *comedy*. Then the next play would be far more peaceful with a few scattered laughs and yet it would be called a *tragedy*.

Finally I got up enough guts after class one day to ask the prof. She explained it this way: "Every play is classified in one of these two groups; it is either a comedy or tragedy. The comedy is any play, regardless of what happens throughout, that ends on a positive note for the hero or heroine. The tragedy is any play that ends on a negative note for the hero or heroine. It is the ending that determines the category." That made sense.

This same principle applies to the drama of life. Every life is either a tragedy or comedy. For a Christian, no matter how many struggles and disappointments we face along the way, our lives are comedies because we know that they will always end right. Life for a non-Christian, however, no matter how exciting it might seem along the way, will always end a tragedy.

The Ultimate Awards Assembly The truly successful person might have ups and downs along the way, but in the end he gets the prize.

Awards assemblies can either be fun or frustrating, depending on whether you are a participant or just a spectator. At the end of the high-school year there is hardly a moment as exciting as hearing your name called over the loudspeaker, with the entire student body listening. The crowd approval is worth more than the trophy or varsity letter. Likewise, there is nothing quite as humiliating as silently sitting there feeling like a nerd.

God never wants us to forget that He is hosting an awards assembly that will end all awards assemblies. Varsity jackets wear out, trophies break and collect dust, but there is nothing perishable about the reward Jesus will give us. While it is exciting to hear our names over the P.A. system at the end of the school year, imagine what it will be like to hear our names mentioned in the throne room of God. We step up front and center, the grandstands of heaven are looking on, Jesus takes us by the hand, smiles and says, "Well done, my good friend and welcome to paradise." Your goose bumps will be the size of blisters.

I can assure you, all the mockers who tried to trip us up will be silenced. All the tears we cried and all the sweat we dripped will be more than compensated for. All our little sacrifices will seem like nothing in light of the One who sacrificed everything for us. That movie, which will not be filmed until sometime tomorrow, needs to be shown over and over again in our brains today. What is really important in life is what is important after life.

There will be no swimsuit competition down the golden streets in heaven. There will be no spelling bees, and no tryouts for the choir. There will be no pimples or pot smokers or popularity contests. All the mocking and teasing will be finished. Rather than outward appearances, Jesus will judge us according to our inward appearance. Rather than how successful we made ourselves, Jesus will discover how successful we were at helping others succeed.

A person has never lived who could succeed without Jesus or fail with Him. When the final awards assembly takes place, there will be many surprises. Some of those who won big prizes here will not even get honorable mention there. And many of those who were no-names here will be heroes in heaven. Jesus is the One who makes all the difference. While others might call us *wipeouts,* Jesus will call us *winners.*

Thoughts

1. In what ways can a teenager "quit" or even "die"?
2. What standards should we use to determine success? What is ultimate success?
3. What is a "moral standard"?
4. What does sacrifice have to do with success?
5. "We can actually determine a person's value system by watching what they are willing to sacrifice." Explain.
6. What lesson can we learn from Shakespeare's plays about life and success?
7. List six different characteristics of heaven.
8. What does it mean to live for God's approval?

Feelings

1. Describe some of the emotions involved when you know you have been forgiven.
2. What are some things of value Jesus might ask us to sacrifice? Have you ever sacrificed anything for Him? What?
3. Whose approval means the most to you?
4. Describe what it would be like for Jesus to look you right in the eye, smile, and say, "Welcome, my friend, this is paradise!"

Appendix: A Closer Look in the Book

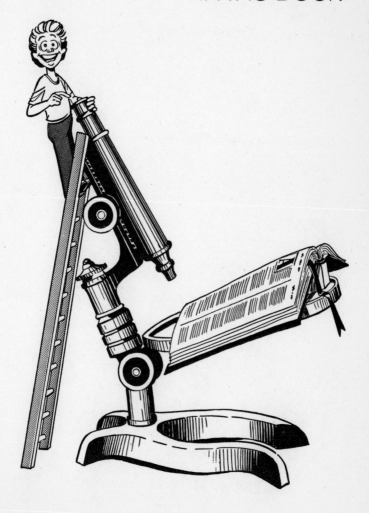

Chapter 1

Read Exodus 3 and 4.

1. Essentially, what is God asking Moses to do?

2. How would you feel if you were Moses?

3. Almost every time God spoke, Moses objected to it. List every time you find Moses objecting. Look for the word *but*. You should find four or five!

   - _____
   - _____
   - _____
   - _____
   - _____

4. Moses finally tells God he doesn't want the assignment (4:10). Why? What personal insecurity did Moses have?

5. What truth did God point out to Moses (4:11, 12)?

6. How did Moses respond to God's encouragement (4:13)? How should he have responded?

7. Was God pleased with Moses' response (4:14)?

8. Do you have some area of your life, as Moses did, that makes you feel insecure about yourself? How does what God told Moses in 4:11, 12 apply to you? How does God expect you to respond?

Chapter 2

Mocking Others
Read Matthew 7:1–5.

1. Here we see Jesus dealing with a common problem—criticism. According to v. 3, what does our criticism of others tell us about ourselves? (When we see a speck in someone else's eye, what does it say about our own eye?)

2. "The worse a person feels about himself, the more critical he will be of others." Respond.

3. According to these verses, what can distort our view of others?

4. In v. 5, what does it mean to "first take the log out of your own eye"? How will this help us to see others clearly?

When We Get Mocked
Read Matthew 5:38–48.

1. Anyone can be friends with those who are friendly. But we all need to know what to do when our friends are *not* friendly. How does what Jesus says contradict the typical response?

2. Not only are we told to give what is taken away, but we are encouraged to voluntarily give even more. If we follow this advice, how will it help us to feel good about ourselves? Does this apply to responding to criticism? How?

3. Should the way others treat us determine the way we feel about ourselves? What should determine the way we feel about ourselves?

Chapter 3

Read Matthew 6:25–34.

1. List everything we are told *not* to be anxious about.

2. Define *anxious.*

3. Why does Jesus tell us not to worry about all these areas? What do they have in common?

4. What do we learn about responsibility from birds (v. 26)? from the lilies (vv. 28–30)?

5. Specifically, why are we told not to worry about our body (v. 25)? Ultimately, whose responsibility is our body (our looks, our height, our intelligence)?

6. In verses 32 and 33, Jesus contrasts the desires of the non-Christian with the desires of the Christian. Explain the difference.

7. God has given us certain responsibilities, and other things were never intended to be our responsibility. Based on this teaching of Jesus, what areas are *not* our responsibility and what one major area *is* our responsibility?

Chapter 4

Read Psalm 139.

1. What qualities of God are emphasized in:
   a. vv. 1–6 _____
   b. vv. 7–12 _____
   c. vv. 13–18 _____
   d. vv. 19–24 _____

2. How do each of these qualities affect the way we should feel about ourselves?
   a. _____
   b. _____
   c. _____
   d. _____

3. Which verses indicate that God knows where we will live?

4. Which verses indicate that God knows who our parents will be?

5. Which verses indicate that God knows what our physical bodies will look like?

6. Which verses indicate that God knows what skills and talents we will have?

7. Which verses indicate that God knows we have no reason to hide anything from Him?

8. Describe how these verses make you feel about yourself. About God.

127

Chapter 5

Read Isaiah 45:9–11.

1. In verse 9, to which craftsman does God compare Himself? What implication does this have in terms of God's activity?

2. In verse 10, to which family member does God compare Himself? What implication does this have in terms of God's dealing with us?

3. According to Ephesians 2:10, how are we described?

4. What is it inside of people that causes us to resist, resent, even hate some of God's design in our lives?

5. Clay goes through many stages before it becomes a useful vessel. Relate each of these phases to God's dealings with us as our Master Potter.
    a. Being dug from the miry bog
    b. Being pounded
    c. Being formed into a vessel
    d. Being fired in the furnace
    Have you experienced each of these phases? Which is the most difficult—the easiest to resent? Which is the most important?

6. What does resenting our parents have to do with our relationship with God? With ourselves?

7. What does it mean to be "clay in God's hands"?

128

Chapter 6

Read Ephesians 4:11–16.

(This is difficult to understand the first time because it is two long, complicated sentences. Read it through three times.)

1. According to these verses, "when we grow up," who will we look like?

2. What are several characteristics of maturity mentioned here?

3. What five gifts/offices are listed in verse 11? Define and distinguish.

4. What are their purposes (v. 12)?

5. What is "a saint"?

6. Why is Christ called "the Head"?

7. In contrast to these verses, in what ways do you consider yourself mature? Immature?

For further study look up "idols/idolatry" in a concordance, especially Exodus 20:3–6 (the first two commandments) and discuss the following:

1. Can teen idols cause us to break these commandments? How?

2. Specifically, which teen idols might be popular *but* dangerous?

3. What standards would be helpful in screening our "heroes"?

Chapter 7

Read 2 Samuel 11 and 12.

1. Which two major sins did David commit?

2. When David learned about the result of his first sin—Bathsheba's pregnancy—what was his immediate response? What was he attempting to do (11: 6–13)? Did his plan succeed?

3. What was his counterplan?

4. In a sense, he got away with his scheme with everyone *but* God. (Read the last sentence in chapter 11). God sent His prophet Nathan with what message?

5. What was the point in 12:12?

6. How did David respond?

7. What was the lasting consequence of David's sin?

Psalms 32 and 51 were written by David during this period of his life. Read Psalm 32.

1. When David hid his sin, was he happy (vv. 3, 4)?

2. What brought real happiness to him (vv. 1, 2, 5)?

3. How do the "horse and mule," "bit and bridle" remind us of David's experience (vv. 8, 9)?

Chapter 8

Read 1 Samuel 15.

1. Describe Saul's physical appearance (9:2).

2. Describe Saul's spiritual appearance (10:1, 6–7, 9–10).

3. How did Saul disobey the specific word of God (15:9)?

4. Despite his disobedience to God, how did Saul feel about himself (15:12, 13)?

5. Even after Samuel confronted him, how did Saul respond (15:20)?

6. Who did he blame for the disobedience (15:21)?

7. When Saul finally admits his error, what was the *cause* of his downfall (15:24)?

8. After Saul is utterly rejected by God, he still chooses man's approval (15:30). How can we tell?

9. What principle did Saul fail to identify in 16:7?

10. In one sentence, state the message of this story for each of us.

Chapter 9

Read Luke 16:14-31.

1. Who are the two main characters in this drama? What do they represent?

2. How was their situation reversed in the afterlife?

3. Is there any way to escape from hell once you are there (v. 26)?

4. How are we warned how to spend our lives (v. 29)?

5. About whom was Jesus telling this parable (v. 14)?

6. What was the real problem that the Pharisees had (v. 15)?

7. Who would you rather be, Lazarus or the rich man?
   What values does your choice represent?
   Who would have been considered a "success" by the townspeople?
   Who was the success in God's eyes?

8. Who do you know like Lazarus?

9. The rich man must have walked past Lazarus several times a week, looking down on him. Now he is looking up to him. Whom are you guilty of looking down on? How should you look at needy people? What values would need to be reversed?